A Young Man's Guide to Making Right Choices

JIM GEORGE

HARVEST HOUSE PUBLISHERS

EUGENE, OREGON

Cover by Dugan Design Group, Bloomington, Minnesota

Cover photos © Artpose Adam Borkowski / Shutterstock; si.re-flex / Fotolia

A YOUNG MAN'S GUIDE TO MAKING RIGHT CHOICES
Copyright © 2011 by Jim George
Published by Harvest House Publishers
Eugene, Oregon 97402
www.harvesthousepublishers.com

Library of Congress Cataloging-in-Publication Data
George, Jim, 1943-
A young man's guide to making right choices / Jim George.
    p. cm.
ISBN 978-0-7369-3025-3 (pbk.)
ISBN 978-0-7369-4227-0 (eBook)
1. Christian teenagers—Religious life. 2. Teenage boys—Religious life. I. Title.
BV4541.3.G467 2011
248.8'32—dc22

                                                                2010052975

Printed in the United States of America

11 12 13 14 15 16 17 18 19 / BP-NI / 10 9 8 7 6 5 4 3 2 1

Contents

Making the Right Choices

*Choose for yourselves this day
whom you will serve.*

—JOSHUA 24:15

Jason, a typical teen guy, was suddenly jolted out of a deep sleep by the clamor of trash cans being rolled to the street curb. At first he was mad, wondering, *Just who do they think they are making all that racket so early in the morning? Don't they know a busy guy needs his sleep?* Then a second wave of adrenalin hit, this time with fear, as Jason rolled over and looked out his window. *Oh, no! That's Dad doing my chores...again! I'm really in for it this time!*

What time was it anyway? Jason thought as he looked at his alarm clock. *Oh, no, I'm late—way late! Did I forget to set my alarm?* He had planned to get up early to finish his English paper, which was due today! Drat and double drat! There were a lot of things he had planned to do last night—finish his English

5

essay, work ahead on his history paper, maybe catch up on his Bible-reading schedule for his church youth group, and finally get around to writing a thank-you note to his aunt for the birthday money she sent several months ago. (That was his mom's Number One assignment for last night, and he had thought to himself, *No worries; it's waited this long. Maybe tonight, right?* On and on…and on…Jason's "Things I Meant to Do" list went.

But Jason had ended up getting a little sidetracked. And why not? The money his aunt gave him had been well spent…on a new DS game. Well, one challenge level led to another, and before long Jason had battled the "forces of evil" so long on his game (a full hour past the bedtime curfew his parents had sent) that his mom had forcefully interrupted and made him end his simulated life-and-death struggles and turn out his light.

Life Is Full of Choices

Jason had begun his evening with great intentions of making right choices. But something pulled him away from those good intentions. And in the end—actually, the next morning—he began to suffer a landslide of consequences due to those bad choices.

As the section title says above, life is full of choices. And the funny thing about choices is that sometimes the same exact choice might be bad for one guy but okay for another. Take, for example, the simple choice of breakfast food. Jason's friend Marty is trying to make the basketball team. He's a great shot, but he has a problem keeping his weight down, so he needs to be more disciplined about what he eats. Eating several bowls of a certain cereal each morning with lots of milk and sugar would be a huge caloric problem for Marty, but it wouldn't be a problem for Jason because he's as thin as a rail!

Do you realize your choices for each day begin at the end of the *previous* day, when you decide what time you need to get up and then set your alarm? And the next big choice is actually getting up when you hear the alarm clock…which then leads to getting dressed, doing your chores, eating breakfast, and getting to school on time. Your choices continue right on through your day and include doing your homework and being a good family member when you get home, until you set the alarm again at the end of the day.

Yes, life is full of choices. Someone said it well:

> My life is not made by the dreams I dream
> but by the choices I make.[1]

Choices Through the Rearview Mirror

You've probably been to a camp or retreat or youth meeting where there was a "guys' sharing time," a time when those who were brave enough recounted some of the choices they made in their past. It's as if they're looking at their past in a rearview mirror. (If you drive, you know all about looking into the rearview mirror to see what's going on behind you, and if you don't drive, you will one day!) Now, the guys who shared were no longer living back in their past, but they could still see, remember, and taste the consequences of their choices—both the good and the bad. Their sharing may have included phrases like…

> I wandered off the path…
> I became like the prodigal son…

I fell away from the Lord…
I got sidetracked in sin…
I lost my first love…
I strayed from the truth…
I made some wrong decisions…
I went off the deep end…
I got in with the wrong crowd…

I've sat in on a few of these sharing sessions myself, and I couldn't help but wonder, *What happened? How does someone wander off the path, lose their first love for Jesus, stray from the truth, fall off the deep end, or get involved with the wrong crowd?*

Well, we both know what happened, don't we? Somehow, at some time, for some reason, a wrong choice was made. Maybe it was just a little lie. Just a little shading of what's right. Just a little bending of a rule. Eventually, as this happens again and again, there comes a day when making wrong choices became all too easy. And it's usually not until then that a guy realizes his life has become a mess.

Checking Out God's Word

It's one thing to read a book written by an author about a subject, but it's quite another to read the Book—the Bible—written by the Author of all things, God Himself. In this book, I'll share a lot of thoughts and tips with you. Most of them are things I've learned over the years. I'll pass them on to you as a young man who's in the process of making decisions that will shape your future. But the things you should definitely make sure you take to heart and pay the most attention to are the things God Himself tells you in His Word, His Book, the Bible.

When you get to this section in each chapter—entitled "Checking Out God's Word"—you'll find a number of Bible verses. I've included the text of the verses for you so you can read them without having to grab your Bible. I also invite you to mark up the verses and make notes. You don't have to do that if you prefer not to. But don't hesitate to circle certain words and underline things you want to remember. Put a question mark beside anything you wonder about or want to know more about. You can even draw in the margins. I've tried to leave enough space for you to write out your thoughts about what God is saying. Do whatever will help you understand the verses and make them your own. (And of course, it would be a good idea at some time to look up the verses in your Bible.) Here we go, from God's Word to you.

The Israelites made a choice—Joshua, the leader of God's people, asked them to do exactly what we've been talking about—to make a choice. Listen in as Joshua speaks to the people about choosing between serving God and serving false gods. According to the verses below, what choice did Joshua give to the people? And praise God, if you read further in the book of Joshua you will discover that the people made the right choice, choosing to serve God.

> *Fear the LORD and serve Him with all faithfulness…*
> *choose for yourselves this day whom you will serve…*
> *But as for me and my household, we will serve the*
> *LORD* (Joshua 24:14-15).

Lot made a choice—Lot was the nephew of Abraham. Because of the large number of cattle the two men possessed, Abraham asked Lot to choose between two parts of the land. One part was green and with plenty of water—perfect for grazing cattle. The other part was dry hill country and not so perfect. In fact, it was a desert. According to the verses that follow, what was Lot's choice?

> *Lot looked up and saw that the whole plain of the Jordan was well watered...So Lot chose for himself the whole plain of the Jordan and set out toward the east* (Genesis 13:10-11).

Sadly, Lot did not choose wisely. He chose the grassy green pastures—which just happened to be near the two most wicked cities of his day, Sodom and Gomorrah. His choice was based on what looked good. Unfortunately, the consequences of that choice were devastating for Lot and his family.

Joseph made a choice—Joseph was a teenager when his jealous brothers sold him into slavery in Egypt. There, in a strange land, Joseph was all alone without family. In time, his master's wife flirted with him and wanted him to sin with her. After all, nobody was around, she explained. Who would ever know?

How should Joseph respond? Note his choice and the reason for his choice.

> *He refused...[and] told her... "How then could I do such a wicked thing and sin against God?"* (Genesis 39:8-9).

Joseph chose to live his life God's way. He honored God. God then honored Joseph's choice and made him a leader of the land of Egypt and the savior of his family,

Daniel made a choice—Can you imagine being taken prisoner and forcefully moved to a foreign land as a teenager? And once you got there, you were told to turn away from your religious beliefs and to follow instead the ways of those who lived in the pagan land? Well, that's what happened to Daniel. In the place where he was taken, Daniel was told to eat foods that were forbidden by his Jewish background. What pressure! What did he do?

> *Daniel resolved not to defile himself with the royal food and wine, and he asked the chief official for permission not to defile himself this way* (Daniel 1:8).

Daniel chose to live life God's way—not only on this one occasion, but also numerous times during his many years in this foreign land. At every step and every day, God blessed Daniel and promoted him to high positions of leadership.

Things to Remember About Choices

—Attractive choices sometimes lead to sin.

—Good choices have positive long-term results.

—Right choices are sometimes difficult. [2]

Making the Tough Choices

I'm sure you already know your actions are a matter of choice. Sure, some choices are made for you. They are out of your control, and are made by those who are responsible for you…like your parents, your teachers, your coaches, and your youth leaders. But many choices each day—and almost each minute of the day—are yours to make. Do you yet realize that these choices are a matter of your will? You get to decide what you will or won't do, how you will or won't act. You make the choices, which means you can't blame anyone else for what happens next.

As you prepare to make the tough choices, the choices that must be made, can you think of one tough choice you need to make right now? What's holding you back? Peer pressure? Fear? Pride?

Pray young Solomon's prayer right now. He asked God, "Give me wisdom and knowledge" and "Give your servant a discerning heart…to distinguish between right and wrong" (2 Chronicles 1:10 and 1 Kings 3:9). Then make that choice—the one that's keeping you from living your life God's way. Make the right choice, however tough it is to do so.

Things to Do Today to Make Right Choices

- Read again the section "Choices Through the Rearview Mirror." Do any of the comments mentioned in the guys' sharing time fit your life today? If so, talk it over with God. Admit to God any wrong choices you've made. Then ask Him for the wisdom to make the right choices starting right now.

• Read again Joshua 24:14-15 (see "Checking Out God's Word"). As you look at your life today, do you think you are making the kind of choice Joshua and the people made, the choice to serve God and God alone? Why or why not? What first right choice will you make to begin choosing to serve God, to live for Him? Is there something you should be doing, but aren't? Something you know God wants you to do, but you're not? Be honest. The king and warrior David was brutally honest with God. He asked God to…

> *Search me, O God, and know my heart;*
> *test me and know my anxious thoughts.*
> *See if there is any offensive way in me,*
> *and lead me in the way everlasting*
> (Psalm 139:23-24).

• As you have already read, choices are a matter

of your will. You get to decide what you will or won't do, how you will or won't act. Think of two or three things you can do daily that will better prepare you to make right choices. Then, of course, begin doing them.

~~~~~~

Guy to Guy

Jot down three things Jason failed to do that started his day down the road to chaos.

What could you tell Jason to do differently tomorrow?

Of all the verses shared in this chapter, which one meant the most to you, and why?

In what ways are you like Jason, and what new choices do you need to start making?

Would You Like to Know More?
Check It Out

Read Proverbs 1:10-19. What warning is given to the young man in verse 10?

What is the advice given to this teen guy in verse 15?

What is the end result for those who make the choice to participate in evil deeds (verse 19)?

It's your turn to read about Lot's choice. Read Genesis 13:5-11. How is the situation described that made a decision necessary (verses 5-7)?

What did Abraham propose as a solution (verses 8-9)?

What choice did Lot make, and why (verses 10-11)?

Now quickly scan Genesis 19:12-29. What were some of the results of Lot's choice?

What choice was made by two brothers in Matthew 4:18-20?

What choice was made in Matthew 9:9?

Have you made this choice, or do you need to? Be sure to think about it.

God's Guidelines for Making Right Choices

- *Treat each day as being important.* "Teach us to number our days aright, that we may gain a heart of wisdom" (Psalm 90:12).

- *Admit your need for wisdom…and ask for it!* "If any of you lacks wisdom, he should ask God, who gives generously to all without finding fault, and it will be given to him" (James 1:5)

- *Work at developing a deep respect for God.* "The fear of the LORD is the beginning of wisdom, and knowledge of the Holy One is understanding" (Proverbs 9:10).

- *Make sure you have a vital relationship with Jesus.* "I keep asking that the God of our Lord Jesus Christ, the glorious Father, may give you the Spirit of wisdom and revelation, so that you may know him better" (Ephesians 1:17).

- *Be willing to pay any price for the truth.* "Buy the truth and do not sell it; get wisdom, discipline and understanding" (Proverbs 23:23).

Daylight's a Burning!

How long will you lie there, you sluggard?
When will you get up from your sleep?

—PROVERBS 6:9

R emember where we left Jason in the last chapter? In bed!
Can you picture the scene—and the sound? (Maybe you've been there too.) Jason was dead asleep. Totally knocked out. And then there was a terrible noise. It took Jason a moment to realize who and where he was—and what that awful sound was. As consciousness arrived, he shuddered and realized, *Oh no! That's my alarm—already?* Then he thought, *Not another day—ugh!*

Poor Jason was so tired. As you remember, he had stayed up late playing on his DS. His solution? *Maybe I'll snooze for just a few more minutes.* With this lame thought, Jason rolled over and pressed the snooze button one more time.

A Simple but Hard Choice

Is your life getting more hectic and complicated? It usually does as you get older. You have important decisions to make. School work is getting harder and harder. Then there's driver's training and getting a license and all the responsibility that goes with that. And money becomes crucial—making it, saving it, and spending (or not spending) it carefully.

But there's one really simple yet hard choice you've got to make every day. In fact, it's the first choice you need to make every day, whether you realize it or not. That choice is, will you get up when you need to…or not?

Each morning, when your sleep is shattered like Jason's was, realize that it's right then and right there that you have the opportunity to make a choice that will have an impact on the rest of your day. It goes like this: If you get up when you are supposed to, you are more in control of yourself and your day. (Well, at least you're more in control of how it begins. You have to leave room for God's plans and for unexpected interruptions, surprises, and crises.) When you do make the choice to get up at the right time, you are calling the shots from Minute One. You are in the driver's seat of your day.

As we work our way through this book about making right choices, you'll see this one singular choice preparing the path for the rest of each day. You'll see how Choice #1 affects Choice #2…and #3…and #4. It's like the game of dominoes, which is usually played with 28 pieces that must be matched end-to-end. Maybe you've seen a set of dominoes. And maybe you've tried to stand all of the pieces in a line. If so, you probably also know that a shaky hand or bump to the table can cause one domino to topple, which, in turn, causes the others to fall in rapid succession. This is what's known as "the domino effect."

I hate to say it, but when you don't get out of bed on time—so that you can get everything done "in a fitting and orderly way" (1 Corinthians 14:40)—the domino effect goes into action and everything you do for the rest of the day will suffer. It's amazing how that one first choice influences everything else you do.

So, what are you going to do? Will you or won't you commit to making the right choice at the beginning of each day?

Big Results Start with Small Steps

I like to do things in small steps. It's easier to accomplish goals that way, and I have a lot more success at finishing whatever I'm attempting. So instead of declaring, "I'm going to get up on time every day for the rest of my life," I simply try to get up on time for just one day. You see, what you are today is what you are becoming. And what you are today is what you will be in the future, if nothing changes. Every act repeated—either good or bad—is creating the real you. Each choice—whether good or bad—made over and over again becomes a habit. And I'm guessing your goal is a lot like mine: to make the right choices over and over again until you established good, godly habits.

And what about your dreams? What do you want to be? What do you want to do? What kind of person do you want to become?

Well, as they said in the Wild West, "Daylight's a burning!" When you get up, you have the opportunity to make your dreams come true. You can get to work on becoming the man God created you to be. And you get to do the cool things He's planned for you. You have all day to make right choices that move you step by step toward something exciting, something excellent, something outstanding, something you can look at and measure as an accomplishment at the end of the day.

And when you don't get up? Well, you probably know the answer to this one all too well! You miss the opportunity to make your dreams happen or to make progress toward them today. I like the truth of this quote I found from a teen magazine: "Oversleeping will never make dreams come true."[1]

So, just for the record, getting up on time is the first right choice you get to make every day. And it's a huge choice!

Checking Out God's Word

God has a lot to say about people who are lazy. The Bible often refers to a lazy person as a "sluggard," as someone who has a bad habit of being lazy, slow, or idle. A sluggard is anyone who hates to get up and hates to work. If you've ever seen a slug move slowly across a sidewalk or driveway, then you get the picture. As you read these verses, remember to feel free to interact with them. (For instance, I'm eying the two question marks below… and a consequence.) Or just enjoy reading them.

> *How long will you lie there, you sluggard? When will you get up from your sleep? A little sleep, a little slumber, a little folding of the hands to rest—and poverty [ruin] will come on you like a bandit* (Proverbs 6:9-10).

As a door turns on its hinges, so a sluggard turns on his bed (Proverbs 26:14).

Facts About a Sluggard

1. He will not begin things.
2. He will not finish things.
3. He will not face things. [2]

Meet Some People Who Got Up on Time... or Even Sooner!

As you go through this section, feel free to mark up the verses and make notes in the margins about what you are learning. Or just let their words sink into your heart and motivate you. Each of these people has a loud message for you.

Jesus—God's Son and our Savior got up early. What is one thing He did once He was awake?

> *Very early in the morning, while it was still dark, Jesus got up, left the house and went off to a solitary place, where he prayed* (Mark 1:35).

Jesus talked to His heavenly Father first thing in the morning. He prayed to God. What happened when He prayed? He tapped into God's wisdom and power for doing His will for one more day—the day in front of Him. When Jesus finished praying, He was armed for facing and handling all kinds of temptation, as well as enjoying all the good things that would happen that day.

Abraham—This man was the father of the Jewish nation and "was called God's friend" (James 2:23). Believe me, Abraham was a man of prayer. Throughout the book of Genesis, you can see him talking with God again and again. On one occasion he invested a great deal of time begging God to spare his nephew, Lot, from the destruction of Sodom and Gomorrah (see Genesis 18:23-33). Afterward Abraham followed up with God regarding his prayer request to see what the outcome would be. We read this about him:

> *Early the next morning Abraham got up and returned to the place where he had stood before the LORD* (Genesis 19:27).

David—This former sheepherder became a powerful warrior and fearsome king. Yet he never thought it was unmanly to pray and talk to God. In fact, David delighted in worshiping the Lord and thought it was foolish not to seek God's strength and guidance and wisdom. What do you learn about David and prayer in this verse?

In the morning, O LORD, you hear my voice; in the morning I lay my requests before you and wait in expectation (Psalm 5:3).

God's people have been getting up early for thousands of years. They took each day seriously. And they took their work seriously. And they took their worship seriously. Do you think they were tired? Of course. Yet they pressed on with their mission, with the work God had for them to do and with their responsibilities at work. What if they had turned on their hinges on their beds each morning? What if they had made excuses? What if they had slept in?

Hudson Taylor was a man who got up early. He is also the man many church historians point to as having a major influence in bringing Christianity to China. He faced many hardships there, living a life of great sacrifice as he labored to establish numerous mission stations and bring the people to Christ. It's been said of him that he reported that "the sun has never risen over China that I was not already praying for her." Now, that's early rising…and some serious praying!

Teens Who Get Up

I'm amazed every time I read about teens who have such a serious or intense passion for something that it gets them out of bed. For instance (and this is where your dreams come in!), every two years we get a chance to see the best of the best in the

Olympics. Many of the competitors are teens just like you. And there they are, on a world stage, accomplishing major feats of strength, agility, and speed. How did they get there? How did they grow to excel? By training. By practicing. By taking advice and following instructions. And, of course, by getting up early in the morning to do all of this plus go to school and do their homework. These teens did this because they were following a dream—a dream powerful enough to get them out of bed each day so they could do what was necessary to reach their goal.

Teens roll out of bed for all kinds of reasons. To train for sports, to meet with a prayer group, or to gather for prayer at the school flagpole. To work on their Bible study for youth group. To meet with a study group at school. To go over exam material one more time before a test.

What is it you are passionate about? What is it you like doing more than anything else? What would you like to be doing but never seem to have enough time for? If you get a chance, take a minute to jot down an answer or two.

A Journey of a Thousand Miles Begins with a Single Step

This well-known saying tells us a lot! It's the perfect advice for making your dreams about the future come true, and it's a great way to fulfill the responsibilities that make up your present daily life. To begin your journey of fulfilling your dreams and taking care of your responsibilities, you must begin with one single step—get up tomorrow. Which brings up the following questions:

> *What do you want to do tomorrow?* This question has to do with your goals and dreams. One of my grandsons wants to have time to learn karate. He also wants to gain a better understanding of computers. Another grandson loves to play tennis and can't wait for his next lesson. What about you? To want something means to desire it strongly. What do you strongly desire to achieve tomorrow that is related to the future you dream of? You can answer this question here or in a notebook or journal. Just name your goal and write out why it's important to you.

> *What do you have to do tomorrow?* This question has to do with taking care of your responsibilities, such as schoolwork, chores, a part-time job. What's on your must-do list? Finishing your English paper? Preparing a handout for a meeting? Taking out the trash for mom? Feeding the dog next door while your neighbors are on vacation? Take a stab at writing a list. WARNING: This list can

get quite long…and it should be! You may need to write it in two columns.

Making the Tough Choices

Here's one of my favorite quotes about living each day with passion. I'm hoping and praying it speaks to you too. It's from the book *Don't Waste Your Life*. (That's quite a title, isn't it?)

> Most people slip by in life without a passion for God, spending their lives on trivial diversions, living for comfort and pleasure…[Don't] get caught up in a life that counts for nothing…Learn to live for Christ, and don't waste your life![3]

Life is a precious gift from God. On top of the life He's given you, He also has incredible plans and purposes for you as well. Nothing could be worse than a life that counts for nothing! You have all the opportunities in the world to live with passion, to make a difference, to contribute to others, and to bring honor and glory to God. God will take you as far as you want to go, as fast as you want to go. Now the tough choice you have to make each day is to get up so you can take the steps that lead you forward day by day on your journey of living—really living—for Christ. Don't waste your life! Get moving toward your goals and dreams.

Things to Do to Make Right Choices

As you think about living your life God's way, let the following choices pave the way for a better tomorrow. This exercise will help you follow through on your first step toward a better life—getting out of bed.

- Step 1: Decide when you need to get up.
- Step 2: Determine when you must get up to make your day go the way you'd like.
- Step 3. Set your alarm…a good loud one. An obnoxious one!
- Step 4: Get to bed at a reasonable time so you can get the rest you need before your wake-up time.
- Step 5: Pray. Ask for God's help in getting up. Tell Him why it's important for you to rise and shine tomorrow. Go over your plans, purpose, commitments, and dreams for tomorrow with Him. Go ahead. He cares, even more than you do!

- Step 6: Purpose to get up—no matter what. Don't give in. And don't worry about not getting enough sleep. It's only for one morning.

- Step 7: Praise God when you hear the alarm. As the new dawn comes forth, cry out with the psalmist, "This is the day the LORD has made; let us rejoice and be glad in it" (Psalm 118:24).

Guy to Guy

No one is a lost cause…including Jason, and including you. Jot down several things Jason failed to do that started his day down the road to chaos.

What could you tell Jason to do differently tomorrow to get out of bed and start his day right?

Of all the verses shared in this chapter, which one meant the most to you that you could pass on to Jason?

In what ways are you like Jason, and what do you need to do to get outta that bed tomorrow?

Would You Like to Know More?
Check It Out

Read Proverbs 6:6-8. "Go to the ant" now. What big lesson do you learn from this tiny insect that you can remember and copy?

—Verse 7

—Verse 8

If the sluggard follows the instructions of verse 6, what will happen?

Read these proverbs and note the results of being lazy.

—Proverbs 12:27

—Proverbs 26:15

In Proverbs 26:16, what else do you learn about a sluggard?

Read these proverbs that point out a number of lame excuses offered by the foolish and lazy sluggard. Also note the results of his excuses.

—Proverbs 20:4

—Proverbs 26:13

What do you learn about the lifestyle of a sluggard in these verses?

—Proverbs 13:4

—Proverbs 21:25-26

By contrast, what does Proverbs 13:4 say is the reward of a diligent lifestyle?

God's Guidelines for Making Right Choices

- *Your future starts as soon as you get up.* "Do not love sleep or you will grow poor; stay awake and you will have food to spare" (Proverbs 20:13).

- *Get up...and keep it going.* "Go to the ant, you sluggard; consider its ways and be wise!" (Proverbs 6:6). "How long will you lie there, you sluggard? When will you get up from your sleep?" (verse 9).

- *Remember the value of a day.* "Teach us to number our days aright, that we may gain a heart of wisdom" (Psalm 90:12).

- *Have goals for each day.* "Not that I have already obtained all this, or have already been made perfect, but I press on to take hold of that for which Christ Jesus took hold of me" (Philippians 3:12).

- *Look to Jesus as your model.* "Very early in the morning, while it was still dark, Jesus got up, left the house and went off to a solitary place, where he prayed" (Mark 1:35).

Getting Your Marching Orders

The law of the LORD is perfect, reviving the soul.
The statutes of the LORD are trustworthy,
making wise the simple.

—PSALM 19:7

I t's now well past time for Jason to get ready for school. We left Jason turning over and hitting the snooze button for the third time…when he should have been hitting the floor. Life, as always, has gone right on without him. Everyone is up and running—except Jason. Which means his mother is now barging into his room with a look of irritation on her face and asking, "Why aren't you up and dressed? You're holding up the whole family!"

Quick, think fast, Jason tells himself as he wipes the sleep from his eyes. With a plan in mind, he blurts out, "There must be something wrong with my alarm clock. I set it [which was true], but somehow it didn't go off [which we know wasn't true]. Mom, you need to buy me a new one." Then for his final defense, Jason blurts out, "Why didn't you wake me? You know I have a big day at school!" With this, Jason's mother throws her hands up in exasperation and walks out of the room.

Whew, thought Jason, *that was a close one.* As he staggers out of bed, he notices his Bible on the nightstand along with the study book the guys in his group were going through. *Oh no, not again! I didn't finish my lesson for tonight's study at church.* Jason let out a sigh. *Oh well, no biggie. Right now I've got more important things to deal with. I'm late for school. Maybe I can finish my Bible lesson during history class. Mr. Brown is soooo boring!*

First Things First

I hope right now you're remembering Choice #1, the one that starts every day off right. That choice is getting up on time so you can do the things you must do and want to do.

And now here we are at Choice #2—*Spend time with God.* Yes, that's right. Have a quiet time. This step will really set the tone of your day…and your voice…and your words…and your actions… and your attitudes…and the way you treat people—starting right at home with your family. So once you're up, you want to make God your number one priority. You want to choose to put first things first. You want to meet with Him before the day gets rolling. It's just like Jesus tells us: "Seek first his kingdom and his righteousness," and "Love the Lord your God with all your heart and with all your soul and with all your strength and with all your mind" (Matthew 6:33 and Luke 10:27).

Do you ever think to yourself that you just don't have time

to stop and spend a few moments with God? I mean, you're a busy guy. You've got a life to live! You have people to see, places to go, and things to do. But oh how wrong we are when we think like this. The Bible is a special book. In fact, it's the greatest book ever written. And if you're a Christian, you are a soldier in God's army. And like any other soldier, your commanding officer—God—wants to give you your orders for the day. Those orders come directly to you through God's Spirit—the Holy Spirit—who speaks to you as you read God's Word.

That's why it's so important to spend time reading God's Word, the Bible. When you read it you will think differently. You will live differently. You will grow spiritually. And you will be blessed. Surely these benefits and blessings—and more!—are worth the simple effort of getting up a few minutes early so you can get into God's Word.

Checking Out God's Word

As you read these verses, note (with your pen, if you want) what is said about God's Word.

The Bible keeps you from bad behavior—*I have hidden your word in my heart that I might not sin against you* (Psalm 119:11).

The Bible leads you in the right direction—*Your word is a lamp to my feet and a light for my path* (Psalm 119:105).

The Bible guides you in the truth—*All Scripture is God-breathed and is useful for teaching, rebuking, correcting and training in righteousness* (2 Timothy 3:16).

The Bible prepares you to serve others—*...so that the man of God may be thoroughly equipped for every good work* (2 Timothy 3:17).

The Bible sharpens your discernment, or judgment—*The word of God is alive and active. Sharper than any double-edged sword.... it judges the thoughts and attitudes of the heart* (Hebrews 4:12).

The Bible gives instructions for eternal life—*The holy Scriptures…are able to make you wise for salvation through faith in Jesus Christ* (2 Timothy 2:15).

Things to Do Today to Get into God's Word

Wow! Now can you see why making the choice to spend time with God in His Word is so important? Getting into the Bible and having a quiet time gives you your marching orders for the day and guides you through it. It also puts your spiritual growth on the fast track. And it helps you know how to follow Jesus' example. How do all these things happen? The answer? It's an inside job. The Bible actually changes your heart.

Take a minute to answer these questions about your life as a teenager.

___ Do you need more confidence?

___ Are you wondering about your future?

___ Are you looking for a few good friends?

___ Are you tired of doing the wrong thing?

___ Are you fed up with failing?

___ Are you bored with your life or do you feel like you're in a rut?

___ Would you like approval from your parents?

Well, I've got great news for you! Do you realize that time in God's Word helps you to know success in every one of these areas...and more? So what can you do to make sure you don't miss out on the miracle of a spiritual workout every single day? Here are a few steps you can take to get started—or to help you keep growing—toward a better understanding of the Bible and turning your life around. When you take these steps each day, you are making the choice to put time with God as a top priority—your Number One priority.

- Step 1: Read it. Just start somewhere. The only wrong way to read the Bible is not to read it.

- Step 2: Study it. Dig in. It's as easy as reading this book, perhaps with a pencil in your hand so you can take notes. Once you get hooked, ask your parents for a teen study Bible. (And be prepared to catch them as they faint!) You can also ask someone to help you find ways to get more out of your Bible time—maybe your dad, or your youth pastor.

- Step 3: Hear it. Church is a big must. And getting to youth group is right behind it. Go wherever you need to go to hear God's Word taught and explained so you can apply it to your life.

- Step 4: Memorize it. (More about this in a minute!) There's no better way to live God's way than to have His Word in your heart and mind...and live it out! If His Word is in you, God will use it in your life. The Bible is part of the armor a soldier for Christ (that's you!) puts on every single day (see Ephesians 6:13-17). It's your sword. Don't do anything without it.

- Step 5: Desire it. You already know the importance of physical food. In fact, you probably can't get enough of it! Well, you need to see the spiritual food of the Word in the same way you view your physical food. It's good for you. It's filling. It's satisfying. And it's necessary for spiritual health and growth. Job said this about God's Word: "I have treasured the words of his mouth more than my daily bread" (Job 23:12).

Before you move on, glance through these steps again and check the one you need to get to work on.

The Best Kind of Studying

If you're a Christian, it makes sense that you'd want to learn as much as you could about Jesus Christ and his Word...Think about it—of all the things you learn in your life, what's the most important? It's not algebra or biology! Although studying these subjects is important and necessary, the most important thing is to know who God is and what He wants you to do in your life. And the more you learn about Him, the more you feel secure and have strength for whatever challenges you have to face. Reading the Bible is the best kind of studying![1]

A Word About Memorizing Scripture

If you're like most teens, you have no problem at all memorizing the lyrics to your favorite songs. I see guys listening to music all the time. And I hear them singing along as they're walking down an aisle in a store. The words are stored in their minds and coming out of their mouths. Well, that's how easy and natural memorizing God's Word can be, if you choose to make it a part of your life.

When you get to the exercises at the end of this chapter, you'll notice God telling Joshua to "meditate" on His Word "day and night" (Joshua 1:8). This means God expected Joshua to know His Word by heart so it (and not the lyrics to a song) was working on his mind, guiding his thoughts, influencing his choices, and coming out of his mouth.

The Bible also tells young men to "hide" God's Word in their hearts. Why? So they won't sin against Him (Psalm 119:11). When you have the Bible in your heart, it serves as a safeguard against sin, against making wrong choices, and against suffering the painful and shameful consequences that go along with making wrong choices.

The young teen woman, Mary, who became the mother of our Savior, Jesus, was passionate about memorizing portions of the Bible. How do we know this? Because Mary was a girl who treasured and pondered God's Word in her heart. When she opened her mouth to praise God for the blessing of the Savior, out came Bible verses—she cited at least 15 passages from the Old Testament (Luke 1:46-55). These were verses and truths Mary had memorized on purpose (a choice!) and learned by heart. They became her language. Truly when she opened her mouth, her lips leaked God's Word. And it was His Word in her heart that helped her live out God's plan for her to become Jesus' mother.

Getting Started on Scripture Memorization

Here's a special assignment for you. What is your favorite verse in the Bible? Write it out here and be sure to memorize it. Make it your own! And if you can't think of a verse, use one of the two below to get you started:

My favorite verse is:

Be strong and courageous. Do not be terrified; do not be discouraged, for the LORD your God will be with you wherever you go (Joshua 1:9).

In all your ways acknowledge him, and he will make your paths straight (Proverbs 3:6).

Making the Tough Choices

Just think—the Bible is all yours all the time. And it's the ultimate source of truth and power. God's Word makes its way into your heart. It turbocharges your soul. And it changes your views about yourself, other people, and the things that are happening in your life. Do you want a more rewarding and fulfilling life? Good news! You can have it. Your better life is as close and as easy as making the choice to pick up your Bible each day, open it up, and take a few minutes to let God speak directly to you. When you do this, you'll know what to do and how to handle everything that comes along in life. You'll receive your marching orders.

Guy to Guy

Jot down three things Jason failed to do that started his day down the road to chaos.

What could you tell Jason about the importance of meeting with God and the difference it can make in his behavior?

Of all the verses shared in this chapter, which one meant the most to you that you could pass on to Jason?

In what ways are you like Jason, and what new choices do you need to start making?

Would You Like to Know More?
Check It Out

Read Psalm 19:7-11. In each verse, note the different terms or words used to speak of the Bible. Also, write out how the Bible is described and its effect on those who read it.

	Term	Description	Effect
Verse 7			
Verse 8			
Verse 9			
Verse 10			

Verse 11—What benefits belong to the one who listens to and keeps God's Word?

Read Joshua 1:7. What are God's commands regarding His Word? As you read, remember that "success" is God's blessings poured out on you because of your obedience. He blesses you when you live your life His way.

—

—

When you do as God says, what will you experience?

Now read Joshua 1:8. What are God's commands regarding His Word?

—

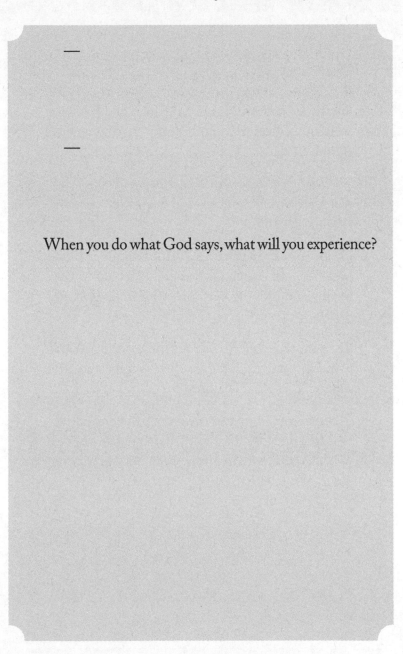

—

—

When you do what God says, what will you experience?

God's Guidelines for
Making Right Choices

- *The Bible keeps you from sin.* "I have hidden your word in my heart that I might not sin against you" (Psalm 119:11).

- *The Bible points you in the right direction.* "Your word is a lamp to my feet and a light for my path" (Psalm 119:105).

- *The Bible gives you answers.* "All Scripture is God-breathed and is useful for teaching, rebuking, correcting and training in righteousness" (2 Timothy 3:16).

- *The Bible works on the heart.* "The word of God is living and active...it judges the thoughts and attitudes of the heart" (Hebrews 4:12).

- *The Bible is your greatest treasure.* "[The Scriptures] are more precious than gold, than much pure gold; they are sweeter than honey, than honey from the comb" (Psalm 19:10).

Knowing the Game Plan

In everything,
by prayer and petition, with thanksgiving,
present your requests to God.

—PHILIPPIANS 4:6

Hallelujah—Jason is up! Whew. As he stands by his bed staring at his Bible and his completed Bible study lesson on the nightstand, he enjoys a wave of satisfaction…until it occurs to him that he's failed miserably in fulfilling his commitment to pray every day this week. He hadn't really wanted to go so far as to make this commitment, but all his friends in the church group had done it, so he went along with them. They were studying about prayer and wanted to put into practice what they were learning. So they made a pledge to pray each day for one week.

"What was I thinking? I can't believe I did that!" mutters Jason. "What a waste of time. Everything's going okay in my life.

So why do I need to pray? And for who…and what? Missionaries I don't know? And sure, family's important, but I'm not so sure about praying for Willard and Heather. Even though they're my brother and sister, they're such a problem at times!" Then with a sigh Jason said, "Okay, God, here goes. Bless the missionaries and my family today, even Willard and Heather—and of course bless me! Amen. Oh, and Mom and Dad too."

God calls us to pray and think and dream
and plan and work—not to be made much of,
but to make much of Him in every part of our lives.[1]

—JOHN PIPER

God Is Available to You—24/7!

"Is that your cell phone ringing?" You hear people ask this every day, don't you? Everyone seems to have a cell phone, and most people have one with countrywide coverage. There are very few places where you can't receive a cell phone signal.

In many ways your prayer life is like a cell phone—you can pray anytime you want, anywhere you want, for as long as you want. But unlike a cell phone, prayer has no fees or additional charges. You also never have to scroll through a directory to find God's number. And your communication with God requires no earpiece—it's "hands free." You have a direct line to the God of the universe 24/7—24 hours a day, 7 days a week. How's that for technology? Divine technology, that is.

10 Reasons God's People Don't Pray

With prayer being as easy as bowing your head and simply talking your life over with God, you'd think that we'd pray a lot more than we do. Have you ever thought about why you don't pray more? You probably have, and so have I. Quite frequently, in fact! As I look at my own heart and life, I've discovered some reasons—and excuses—that God's people often use for not praying. Have you found yourself using any of these excuses before?

1. Worldliness

Our world affects us more than we think. It exerts a constant pressure on us to conform and live like the world lives—instead of living God's way. And besides, because we have all the food, clothes, and shelter we need, plus family, friends, and lots of fun things to do, we make a big mistake and decide, "Why do I need to talk to God? I've got everything I need without spending my time praying. Besides, praying makes me nervous."

2. Busyness

Another reason we don't pray is because, like Jason, we don't take the time or make an effort to pray. We don't view prayer as a priority, and instead, we fill our time with other things we consider more important. We're so busy we don't even get around to planning ahead so we can include prayer in our daily life.

3. Foolishness

Because we're so focused on things that are foolish, trivial, and meaningless, we fail to pray. Over time, our senses can become dulled to the point that we lose our ability to know the difference between what is good and what is evil. Between what is essential and that which has little or no eternal value. Ever so slowly, more and more of life begins to fall into a "gray area" which we think doesn't require prayer.

4. Distance

We have no problem taking time to talk with our friends. Jason and his friend Jack could talk about football, computer games, and girls for hours—and they do! But what about people Jason doesn't know very well? Forget it! It's the same thing with talking to God. When your relationship with God isn't very tight, you find it hard to talk to Him. You don't know what to say, and you don't feel close to Him or comfortable in His presence. So you don't pray.

5. Ignorance

We're clueless about how prayer works. And we don't understand how it fits into our relationship with God or helps us to make right choices. And because we don't know enough about the Bible, we don't really understand God's love for us and His power to make our lives better.

6. Sinfulness

We don't pray because we know we've done something wrong. In our hearts we know we need to talk to God about it, admit it, confess it, agree with Him that what we did was wrong. But because we feel guilty, we make another wrong choice and put off that heart-to-heart talk with God.

So what should we do about our sins and failures? Make a choice to keep short accounts with God. Deal with sin as it comes up—on the spot—at the exact minute that you slip up and fail. Did you yell at your mom? Tell God that was wrong (and then tell your mom too). Were you mean to your brother or sister? The same thing goes for this too. Did you choose not to take the trash out and depend on Dad instead? Ditto. Admit to

God what you did, and (you guessed it) apologize to Dad. Any lies, laziness, lust, or cheating need to be confessed and cleared with God. Once you have a clean slate with Him, you'll be grateful for His forgiveness and want to talk to Him about everything in your life. He's the one Person who will always listen, always forgive, and always show you the better way to live.

7. Faithlessness

We don't really believe in the power of prayer. That's because we don't know the awesome promises God has made to us about prayer. We don't know about His guarantee to answer our prayers. Therefore we don't think prayer makes any difference. So...we don't pray.

8. Pridefulness

Prayer shows our dependence on God. When we fail to pray, in our pride we're saying that we don't have any needs. Or worse, we're saying, "No thanks, God; I'll take care of myself. I'm good. I don't need You on this one."

9. Inexperience

We don't pray because...we don't pray! And because we don't pray, we don't know how to pray...so we don't pray! We're like a dog chasing after its tail. Our failure to pray is a cycle that leads nowhere.

10. Laziness

Maybe this is the most common reason we don't pray. We simply can't or won't put out the effort to talk to God. Prayer is an act of the will. It's a choice. You have to want to do it…and choose to do it.[2]

Checking Out God's Word

As you read each of the following promises and assurances about prayer, notice God's message to you regarding your life and how prayer helps you live it God's way.

Call to me and I will answer you and tell you great and unsearchable things you do not know (Jeremiah 33:3).

Whatever you ask for in prayer, believe that you have received it, and it will be yours (Mark 11:24).

Let us then approach the throne of grace with confidence, so that we may receive mercy and find grace to help us in our time of need (Hebrews 4:16).

Is any one of you in trouble? He should pray (James 5:13).

If any of you lacks wisdom, he should ask God...and it will be given to him (James 1:5).

Love your enemies and pray for those who persecute you (Matthew 5:44).

If we confess our sins, [God] is faithful and just and will forgive us our sins and purify us from all unrighteousness (1 John 1:9).

Here's a caution!—*You do not have, because you do not ask God. When you ask, you do not receive, because you ask with wrong motives, that you may spend what you get on your pleasures* (James 4:2-3).

Making the Tough Choices

A Prayer Checklist

Prayer is a spiritual activity, and, like all other activities, prayer takes a decision and requires effort. So, if you're not praying—or not praying very much—run through this checklist:

- *Check your relationship with God.* Is there something that's caused a barrier between you and God? If so, admit it to Him. Ask God to help you do whatever it takes to deal with the obstacles that stand between you and an open relationship with Him, one that enables you to talk to Him about anything and everything—including making right choices.

- *Check your lifestyle.* What, or who, is influencing you? Is it influencing you positively for the things of God? If not, it's out! Nothing and no one is important enough to endanger your relationship with God and your ability to talk to Him in prayer.

- *Check your desire.* Prayer will never become a strong habit or spiritual discipline if the one main ingredient—desire—is missing. We can know all about what we should do and why we should do it, but if we don't desire to do it, it won't become real in our lives.

Toward a Life of Prayer

Do you want to pray? I'm thinking you do. Here are two simple principles (which give you two more choices!) that will help you move forward in defeating or overcoming your excuses for not praying.

Principle #1

Head to bed. Your goal is to fulfill Choice #1 tomorrow—to get out of bed! All good things begin with this one choice. Well, getting up starts by thinking about it as soon as dinner is over. Finish your homework. Do all your pre-bed stuff. Check your schedule for tomorrow and begin a "To Do" list for it. Be sure your Bible is nearby and your prayer list or notebook is handy in the place where you will (Lord willing) have your quiet time tomorrow. Then go to bed at a reasonable time so you can meet and talk with your heavenly Father in the morning.

And here's an extra reason to head for bed: "sleep experts say most adolescents need eight-and-a-half to nine-and-a-quarter hours of sleep every night. Yet the overwhelming majority of teens (85%) get less than that—on average, about two hours less. The result is that most of today's teens are chronically sleep-deprived. Many are so sleepy that they live in a kind of 'twilight zone.'…the term 'zombie' is a pretty accurate description." [3]

Principle #2

Maybe you've heard the saying, "Something is better than nothing." Any prayer is better than no prayer, right? Some prayer is better than no prayer at all. So start with a choice to pray for at least a few minutes each morning. Graduate little by little to spend more time in prayer.

Guy to Guy

Jot down two or three excuses Jason had for not praying. Also note some of his attitudes.

What could you tell Jason about the importance of prayer and the difference it can make in his life? Or what could you tell him about the difference prayer has made in your life?

Of all the verses shared in this chapter, which one meant the most to you that you could pass on to Jason, and why?

In what ways are you like Jason, and what new choices do you need to make to start making prayer happen?

Would You Like to Know More?
Check It Out

The Bible is filled with people who made the choice to pray about their life and choices. See what you can learn about the difference prayer made in these people's lives and what they talked over with God.

1. David—Read Psalm 32:1-5. What was the issue in David's life, and how did prayer make a difference?

2. Abraham—Read Genesis 18:20-33 and 19:29. What was Abraham's concern, and what did he do about it? What were the results?

3. Jesus—Read Luke 6:12-13. How long did Jesus pray, and what decision did He make afterward? Jot down the decisions you are facing, and then make an appointment on your calendar to pray about them.

4. Jesus—Read Matthew 26:36-44. What was Jesus' intention in verse 36?

How is the seriousness of Jesus' situation described in verses 37-38?

What was Jesus' posture when He prayed (verse 39)?

Jesus was praying about the "cup" of death on the cross. How many times did He pray about doing God's will (verses 39-44)?

What desire was repeatedly expressed in the content of Jesus' prayers (verses 39, 42, and 44)?

After extended time in prayer, how did Jesus proceed to fulfill God's plan that He die for sinners (verses 45-46)?

Nehemiah's Prayer Life

When discouraged, he prayed (1:4).
When seeking direction, he prayed (1:5-11).
When seeking assistance, he prayed (2:1-5).
When under attack, he prayed (4:4-5,9).
When weak and powerless, he prayed (6:9).
When joyful, he prayed (12:27,43).[4]

God's Guidelines for
Making Right Choices

- *Seek to obey God's Word.* "If anyone turns a deaf ear to the law, even his prayers are detestable" (Proverbs 28:9).

- *Let God know about all your concerns.* "God has surely listened and heard my voice in prayer. Praise be to God, who has not rejected my prayer or withheld his love from me!" (Psalm 66:19-20).

- *Always pray in times of trouble.* "The eyes of the LORD are on the righteous and his ears are attentive to their cry...The righteous cry out, and the LORD hears them; he delivers them from all their troubles" (Psalm 34:15,17).

- *Pray instead of worrying.* "Do not be anxious about anything, but in everything, by prayer and petition, with thanksgiving, present your requests to God. And the peace of God, which transcends all understanding, will guard your hearts and your minds in Christ Jesus" (Philippians 4:6-7).

- *Don't forget to pray for others.* "Pray in the Spirit on all occasions with all kinds of prayers and requests. With this in mind, be alert and always keep on praying for all the saints" (Ephesians 6:18).

The Golden Rule Begins at Home

*Do to others as you would
have them do to you.*

—LUKE 6:31

Watch out—Jason's on the move. He's finally out of bed—late! He's already had a run-in with Mom, and now he's on the loose. As he trudges down the hall toward the bathroom, the whole world awaits him, starting with his little brother, Willard. *What a big pain!* Jason thinks. Willard is three years younger than Jason and always makes a complete pest of himself every time Jason's friends come over. *And ugh—there's Heather, who's almost ten. Yeah, Heather thinks she's a princess—and acts like it too.* "She may be a princess, but I'm the king," Jason mutters as he bullies his way down the hall, daring his younger siblings to be foolish enough to get in his way.

Jason acts as if his calling in life is to find ways to make Willard and Heather's lives miserable. And here comes his first opportunity today. Sure enough, his poor brother and sister get the brunt of his waking-up anger as he barks, "Get outta my way! And get outta the bathroom! Can't you see I'm late? Give me some space!" Jason muscles his younger siblings out the bathroom door, slams it in their faces, and locks it. Of course they have to get ready for school too, so they bang on the door and yell for Mom to intervene.

At first glance, it seems like Jason is getting things to work out in his favor. First he got out of taking the trash out ("Good old Dad!"). Then he manipulated and lied to his mother to escape being grounded for getting up late. And now he's pushed his brother and sister out of the bathroom so he can have his own way ("I guess I showed them who's boss around here!").

Checking Out God's Word

I'm sure you've heard of the Golden Rule. Did you know that Jesus was the one who mentioned it first? Below are verses that quote Jesus. Keep in mind as you read them that

these verses are commonly known as the Golden Rule. In many religions, it is stated negatively. "Don't do to others what you don't want done to you." By stating it positively Jesus made it more significant. It is not so hard to refrain from harming others; it is much more difficult to take the initiative in doing something good for them. The Golden Rule as Jesus formulated it is the foundation of active goodness and mercy—the kind God shows to us every day.[1]

After you read the following verses, try writing out a summary of their message to you.

So in everything, do to others what you would have them do to you (Matthew 7:12).

Do to others as you would have them do to you (Luke 6:31).

What You Are at Home Is What You Are

Here's a saying I try to remember at all times: "What you are at home is what you are." And it's true! Think about it for a minute. Why would a Christian act one way out in public—at school, at church, on a sports team—and another way at home? Why would a Christian act one way with friends and another way with family?

The word for this kind of two-faced behavior is *hypocrisy*. It means "phony," and describes a person who is a deceiver and a play-actor. Such an individual is a pretender—one who puts on a mask and pretends to be what he or she is not. It means being one kind of person to some people, and then turning around and being another kind of person to others.

Have you ever known someone who was two-faced, who played the part of two different kinds of people? Or (I hope not, but I have to ask it!), have you acted in a two-faced way? Unfortunately, as you'll soon see, Jason is two-faced. He acts out two roles. He's a modern-day Dr. Jekyll and Mr. Hyde. To his family he's mean, sullen, hard to talk to, and answers only with grunts, shrugs, facial expressions, and hand gestures. But what happens to Jason when he meets up with his friends? He's the man of the hour, high-fiving, flashing smiles, and shouting greetings to everyone. He's as open and happy and helpful as anyone can be. You wouldn't even recognize him. Is this the same guy who makes his family so miserable day after day?

Checking Out God's Word

Fortunately the Bible shows us the right way to treat family members. So read on. Sometimes we learn a lot about our actions by studying their opposites. What do these verses say in contrast to Jason's awful behavior toward his family? You may even want to underline the commands or write a few notes to yourself.

Be kind and compassionate to one another (Ephesians 4:32).

Be imitators of God, therefore, as dearly loved children and live a life of love, just as Christ loved us and gave himself up for us (Ephesians 5:1).

The fruit of the Spirit is love, joy, peace, patience, kindness, goodness, faithfulness, gentleness and self-control (Galatians 5:22-23).

Jesus Changes You from the Inside Out

Have you noticed that many of the choices we've talked about so far have to do with your heart? Basically they involve wanting to live for God. They involve learning what He says about the issues of your life and making the right choices based on what His Word says. And the choice to practice the Golden Rule is no different. The way you talk to others and treat others is a heart issue. How can I say that? Because Jesus said it. Here's how it works:

For out of the overflow of the heart the mouth speaks. The good man brings good things out of the good stored up in him, and the evil man brings evil things out of the evil stored up in him (Matthew 12:34-35).

Do you remember what your life was like before you became a Christian? Can you recall how you acted toward others and treated people? The apostle Paul says you were dead in your sins. You were controlled by the forces of evil. Your actions conformed to a heart of unbelief (Ephesians 2:1-3).

But thank goodness that God, in His great love, showed you mercy, making you alive with Christ. By God's grace, you were saved (Ephesians 2:4-5). And by God's grace, you were also transformed—changed—from the inside out. You are now a new creature in Christ (2 Corinthians 5:17). Therefore, you are to live out what God has put into your heart—the actions of the Holy Spirit (see Galatians 5:22-23 above).

How to Live Out the Golden Rule

It's one thing to know what you should do, and it's another thing to actually do it—to do what helps you to live your life God's way. And that includes how you act toward others at home. With that in mind, here are some choices you can make:

1. *Choose to Have a Spiritual Checkup*

Are you fed up with the way you're living your life and the way you treat people? Then you need Jesus to help you go through a spiritual checkup. Ask yourself: Has my heart been transformed by God from the inside out? Is Jesus really my Savior? Have I truly submitted myself to His leading?

If you answer no to those questions, then you are spiritually dead. Your condition requires a complete spiritual transformation—from the inside out. So begin the process by asking Jesus to come in and take over your heart and your life. You need life as only Jesus can give it. Just a simple earnest prayer will bring you to life spiritually. There's no way in the world you can live like

Jesus and by the Golden Rule if Jesus Christ is not your Savior. Here's a sample prayer you can lift up to Jesus:

> Lord Jesus, I don't know You as my Savior. I am separated from You because of my sin. Forgive me. Come into my life and take control of my actions. I want to follow You. I want to love others. I want to be kind. I want all of the qualities that, according to the Bible, are true of a Christian. Help me turn from my sins and follow Your example. And help me love others as You have loved me. Amen.

2. Choose to Revisit Your Heart

If Jesus is your Savior, then you have the ability to be nice to all people, to treat others in the same way Jesus did. You have His Spirit living in you. So what's the problem? Have you considered there might be unconfessed sin in your heart?

Sin is like filth in a pipe. When there is dirt and garbage in a pipe, it keeps water from flowing through. It's the same way with sin. Sin blocks God's Spirit from flowing through you to produce His best actions and attitudes. Your sin quenches and grieves the Holy Spirit's work in you. That means it's vital for you to choose to confess your sin (1 John 1:9) and allow God to remove all the dirt that is blocking the work He wants to do through your life.

3. Choose to Read Your Bible

The Bible has the power to change you from the inside out. When you make the first choice of your day (after getting up, that is) that of reading your Bible, you'll discover you are not the same. God's Word is pure, powerful, and life-changing. When you read it you will no longer think or act in worldly or bad ways. As you read God's Word you'll discover His Spirit transforming you into a loving, giving son, brother, and person who chooses to treat everyone—especially family—by the Golden Rule, just the way Jesus did (Romans 12:1-2).

4. *Choose to Be Nice at Home*

It may be hard for you to believe this, but there is nothing like family. Friends come and go. Some are fickle and may turn on you. Others may move away or move on to a different group of friends. But your family is forever. One year, five years, ten years, twenty years and more from now, you will still have your family. So invest the bulk of your kindness and goodness at home. Your family members are the people who should matter the most to you. Yes, even your noisy, nosey brothers and sisters! So, how hard is it to be helpful and show kindness to each family member by…

> … choosing to give a cheerful hello in the morning?
>
> … choosing to give a compliment every day?
>
> … choosing to help your little sister clean up her spilled milk?
>
> … choosing to help your little brother find his backpack?
>
> … choosing to give Mom a hand with the groceries?
>
> … choosing to volunteer to help Dad when you see him working around the house or yard?

The Bible says Jesus "went around doing good," and you can too!

Making the Tough Choices

Don't you love it when people practice the Golden Rule and are nice to you? It's a great feeling, isn't it? But unfortunately, it's all too easy to forget to pass the Golden Rule treatment on to others, especially when it comes to our own family members. How many times has your mom or dad told you, "Be nice to your brothers and sisters"? (Or maybe they put it another way: "Why can't you be nice to your brothers and sisters?") Probably more times that you want to admit, right? And what about your parents? They deserve better treatment from you too, don't they? In fact, the Bible tells you to honor, obey, and respect them (Ephesians 6:1-2).

Well, did you know that the Bible never tells you to "be nice"? Now, before you take this literally and run off and act ugly toward someone, let me explain. What the Bible does says is that you are to "be kind" (Ephesians 4:32). You are to "clothe yourselves with compassion, kindness, humility, gentleness and patience" (Colossians 3:12).

What's the difference between being nice and being kind? Being nice only requires that you be outwardly polite. But being kind means that you care about the other person. When you are kind, you are compassionate and considerate. You genuinely care about those around you. It's possible to be nice to another person outwardly yet not like him at all in your heart. But kindness is different. It is deep, intense, and heartfelt. Kindness is for real—it's from the heart.

Yes, but how? you wonder. Your job is simple, but for some strange reason, it's a tough choice to make. You must choose to be kind. You must choose to practice God's Golden Rule—and, again, especially at home. Just think what it would mean to your family if you were the world's best son and brother. Your family members will be blessed, and God will be honored by your thoughtfulness.

Guy to Guy

Jot down two or three ways Jason mistreated his family members. Note too some of his attitudes.

What could you now tell Jason about why and how he should practice God's Golden Rule at home?

Of all the verses shared in this chapter, which one meant the most to you that you could pass on to Jason, and why?

In what ways are you like Jason, and what new choices do you need to start making in relation to your own family...and to people in general?

Would You Like to Know More?
Check It Out

The Bible has much to say about doing to others what you would want done to yourself. They are often referred to as the "one anothers." Several of them are listed below; read them in your Bible. Copy out the main thought—the "one another"—in each verse. Then jot down how you will start applying them in your relationships, starting with your fellow family members. Then jot down how you can apply them to your friends and acquaintances...and even to those who are, in Jesus' words, your enemies (Luke 6:27).

Romans 12:10—

Romans 12:16—

Galatians 5:13—

Ephesians 4:2—

Ephesians 4:32—

Ephesians 5:21—

1 Thessalonians 5:11—

James 4:11—

1 John 3:11—

God's Guidelines for Making Right Choices

- *Don't let anything divide you from your family.* "How good and pleasant it is when brothers live together in unity!" (Psalm 133:1).

- *Become the world's best helper at home.* "Let us not become weary in doing good…Therefore, as we have opportunity, let us do good to all people, especially to those who belong to the family of believers" (Galatians 6:9-10).

- *Never keep back a kindness.* "Do not withhold good from those who deserve it, when it is in your power to act" (Proverbs 3:27).

- *Show you are a Christian by your love.* "Whoever loves his brother lives in the light, and there is nothing in him to make him stumble. But whoever hates his brother is in the darkness" (1 John 2:10-11).

- *Realize God's plan for you is obedience.* "Children, obey your parents in the Lord, for this is right. 'Honor your father and mother'—which is the first commandment with a promise—'that it may go well with you and that you may enjoy long life on the earth'" (Ephesians 6:1-3).

Where's My Favorite T-shirt?

*Whatever you do,
do it all for the glory of God*
—1 Corinthians 10:31

Finally forced to vacate the bathroom by a host of family members, Jason moves down the hall to his room in a huff. "Someday," he mutters, "I'll get out of here and have my own apartment. Then I can take as long as I want in the bathroom!"

As he opens the door to his room with the bold "Keep out or die!" sign on it, he wonders, *Now let's see...what to wear?* Upon entering his room, he's greeted by a disaster zone. Clothes, schoolbooks, CD cases, unfinished projects, and trash are littered everywhere. "Well, no matter. I'm late for school. I'll clean up my room some other time." (How many times has he said those exact words over the past several weeks…or even months?)

Sidestepping several piles, Jason approaches his dresser. As he struggles to get the top drawer open, an earlier choice comes back to haunt him: Rather than fold his T-shirts, Jason had taken the easy way out and simply stuffed the drawer full. And today of all days was the day of reckoning! When he did finally manage to get the drawer open, he saw that every T-shirt was horribly wrinkled. "No matter" Jason reasoned. "Wrinkled is in! Now let me see…where's my favorite T-shirt?"

A moment later, without having tried all that hard to find the shirt, Jason yelled, "Mom, where's my favorite T-shirt? You know, the one with the wild designs?" (The designs were so wild and weird that even Jason found it hard to describe them.)

"Look on the floor of your closet," his mother shouted back from downstairs, "where you keep most of your clothes!"

Sure enough, as he opened the closet door, a huge pile of dirty clothes was staring up at him. Unfortunately this signaled there wasn't much of a selection left to wear to school today. Jason sighed and thought for a moment about his friend Tom. "Why couldn't I have a mom like Tom's? Mrs. Ortiz is a really cool mom. She washes and folds Tom's clothes and keeps his room picked up. Tom always has his favorite T-shirt to wear." Never mind that Jason failed to consider that Tom was an only child and his mom didn't work. By contrast, Jason's mom had three kids—and a full-time job. But as usual, Jason was only thinking of himself. As he contemplated his "unfortunate" life, he saw something in the back of the closet…

"Wait a minute! What's this?" Jason yelped. On a hanger way back in the corner was a T-shirt that his parents didn't like because they weren't sure it met school standards for appropriate attire. Holding his prized find in his hands, Jason muttered, "I don't know what the big deal is about this T-shirt. The words and pictures aren't that bad. And besides, all the guys are wearing T-shirts with edgy messages and pictures."

Jason looked out the window. He saw his mom pulling out of the driveway to take his brother and sister to school and then go to work. *Why not?* he thought to himself. *This is my big chance to wear this blacklisted shirt. If I play this right, I can grab a Pop-tart and be out the door before Dad even gets a look at what I'm wearing. After all, it's only a T-shirt. No big deal! This way I won't stand out so much and be different. And then there's that cute new girl at school. Maybe she'll notice me if I wear this. And so what if I get caught? I can always use the excuse that I had nothing else to wear!*

Clothes Make the Man

Okay, let's talk. Do you realize that what you wear on the outside is a mirror of what's happening (or not happening!) on the inside, in your heart and mind? Jason is about to make a choice regarding what he will wear to school. Sure, it's a small choice on the scale of many other choices a young man has to make. But it's a wrong choice on so many levels! Believe it or not, God desires for you to consult Him about the choices you make every day—even the so-called little ones. In fact, He has a lot to say in the Bible about what you wear. And as a Christian, Jason is—and so are you—God's representative and a walking advertisement for Him.

So what is God's dress code? What are His guidelines when it comes to your clothing? And what does He consider to be a fashion goof? To begin, think about the fact that the Bible gives a lot of instructions about what girls wear. That's because what girls wear is a reflection of their inner character, and God is concerned that they properly represent Him. And even though these instructions are aimed at girls, it shows that God does care about what we wear.

Though the Bible doesn't really comment specifically on what men wear, still, God has His standards. The reason we don't see much stated about men's clothing is because they either dressed for work or war or worship. For them, social and fashion trends were never much of an issue. But based on what God says about Christian character in Scripture, it's possible for us to come up with helpful principles about our clothing choices.

Making the Right Choices

Below are some key words that will help guide you regarding what to wear and not to wear…and when certain types of clothing are appropriate or not.

Moderate—This means not too much, not too little. Moderation indicates that you show some restraint and control over your clothing choices. We could also use the word *modest,* which the dictionary defines as a lack of excesses or pretense or show. To be modest is to wear clothing that is appropriate and proper for a young person—whether a boy or girl—who loves God and wants to follow Him. Modesty is wrapped up in moderation, meaning it avoids extremes. In other words, you should be careful not to wear clothes that have slogans, pictures, or scenes that give a message that would dishonor Jesus in any way.

I work out several times a week in a military gym, and one day I was surprised to see a poster that showed what the guys were and were not to wear while exercising. Most people would probably say, "Who cares? After all, it's just a gym." But even I have to say that some of the guys were getting toward the edge of wearing too little and bordering on being improper, inappropriate, and immodest. Evidently the Army thought so too. That poster was a good reminder to me to be more faithful to remember that wherever I go, I need to dress in moderation and wear what is proper.

Clean (and let's add *neat*)—I realize that most moms do the laundry at home. But you can help out by folding or hanging up your clothes. You can also help by taking a few minutes the night before to choose what you plan to wear. And here's a thought: I was impressed when I heard that the male contestants on the TV show *The Apprentice* all selected, pressed, and ironed their clothes the night before their morning meetings with Donald Trump to get their assignments for the day. If you want to avoid wearing wrinkled clothes, you may want to learn how to use an iron.

Appropriate—What's the occasion? Is it school? Wear some great school clothes. Is it a swim or beach party? Have fun! Is it church? Look your best—worshiping God is involved! Is it your youth group? Grab some really cool (and clean and neat) clothes for hanging out.

Considerate—Throughout the Bible God's people are told to watch out that they don't offend others by what they do. The apostle Paul wrote several times about thinking first of others, even in the matter of the clothes you wear. He tells us "it is better not to eat meat or drink wine or to do anything else that will cause your brother to fall" (Romans 14:21). In another passage he tells us that yes, we are free in Christ, but we are to "be careful, however, that the exercise of your freedom does not become a stumbling block to the weak" (1 Corinthians 8:9). In other words, we are to give up our freedom to wear whatever we want. Instead we are to think first of others and how it might affect them.

Oh, and here's something else to consider. Will girls be there? Girls you want to impress in the right way? Or are you getting ready for a date? A word to the wise: Clothes make the man. So wear your best. The kind of gal you're looking for should be looking for someone with some pretty high standards!

Obedient—Jason was given standards by loving parents, but he was about to step outside them. When your parents give wise advice and you listen to them, several good things happen. One is that you won't end up making foolish choices that could have negative consequences, such as dressing to attract what could be the wrong kind of girl or the wrong kind of crowd. Consider this: Anyone who bases a friendship with you on what you wear or don't wear isn't the right kind of friend for you.

It's important for you to listen to your parents and follow their guidelines. As you've already learned in this book, God wants you to respect your parents, and that includes honoring the standards they set for you. And it's pretty simple: If they don't want you to wear a certain shirt, don't. If they think you should wear something nicer, do it. Also, if you are in a group—a choir, orchestra, band, debate team, chess club, worship team, or whatever—you should wear what your advisor tells you to wear. This is not the time or place to get creative or compromise. The same goes for respecting the standards set by your school. The Bible is crystal clear that you are to submit yourself to governments and authorities (see Romans 13:1-2 and 1 Peter 2:13-14). When you follow your school or group dress code, you represent God and Jesus in a good way and set an example for others.

Ask what to wear—This is an easy one. When it comes to clothing choices, take some time to stop, think, and if necessary, ask. Think first, then dress. Ask yourself, What is the purpose of the event? If it's to honor someone (for instance, an awards ceremony or assembly, graduation, a recital), then honor that person and the occasion by wearing nicer clothing. If it's a party, ask yourself, Who is the host? If some parents are hosting a birthday party for their son or daughter, honor not only the birthday person but also their parents by taking time to look nice. If you have a role in the event (such as reading the Scripture passage during a church service or Sunday school or youth group), raise the level of your clothes to fit the occasion. If pictures are going to be taken (I'm sure you're getting the point by now), dress your best, even if the dress is casual, so you don't draw attention to yourself as the one who looked like he got his clothes out of a dirty clothes basket.

My wife and I are both public speakers, and I also do a lot of preaching at church services. We have a personal policy to always ask what those in attendance will be wearing, what the sponsor or host is planning to wear, and what they would like us to wear. And then we go one step further and dress slightly better than what we are told. I don't remember where I heard this bit of leadership advice, but it has served as a helpful guideline for years: "It is always better to arrive at any event looking slightly better than the norm." That's a great rule of dress.

Unfortunately, today's society isn't interested in moderation or standards. Its motto is the opposite: Anything goes. Push the limits. Express yourself! Who cares anyway? But God calls us away from such thoughts and toward His standards. In Romans 12:2 He pleads with us to live His way, as you'll see in the next section.

Checking Out God's Word

Read Romans 12:2 below. I've broken it down into three parts. It's a verse that points you to the path for living your life God's way and making the choices He wants you to make. If you want, jot down your personal thoughts or "notes to self" as you read about these commands from the Lord.

Do not conform any longer to the pattern of this world. In other words, don't let the world squeeze you, a young man after God's own heart, into its ungodly mold. Don't copy the customs and fashions of this world.

Instead, *be transformed by the renewing of your mind.* Let God remold your mind from the inside. Cooperate with Him and change your outlook and thinking to match the transformation God is working in you. As a Christian, you are His. You belong to Him. And your life should reflect that. You need to live for Him, to live His way. Don't hesitate to turn your back on the world and its ways. Instead, take on the ideals and attitudes of Christ.

And the result? *Then you will be able to test and approve what God's will is—his good, pleasing and perfect will.* In other words, you will be able "to find and follow God's will; that is, what is good, well-pleasing to Him and perfect."[1]

Here are some good questions to ask yourself the next time you reach for a T-shirt or jeans or whatever. What are my motives for wearing these clothes? Is it to conform to the world's ways? Is it to dress like my peers who set the standard for my school or group? Is it to draw attention to myself in some way? Is it to make a statement or send a message? God wants His people of all ages—teens included—to have the highest standards, and that includes being thoughtful about what you wear.

Things to Do Today to Make Right Choices

Now read for yourself some additional principles God wrote to help you choose what you will and will not wear. These guidelines will help you to make right choices—God's choices—about what you wear. You may want to look up each verse in your Bible. What is each passage saying to you?

> Seek God's approval not the world's—*Am I now trying to win the approval of men, or of God? Or am I trying to please people? If I were still trying to please*

men, I would not be a servant of Christ (Galatians 1:10).

Don't follow the crowd; you have a higher standard—*Dear friend, do not imitate what is evil but what is good* (3 John 11).

Develop inner godly character; it's your best outfit!—*But you, man of God...pursue righteousness, godliness, faith, love, endurance and gentleness* (1 Timothy 6:11).

Be careful what you wear; your clothing is sending a message—*So whether you eat or drink or whatever you do, do it all for the glory of God* (1 Corinthians 10:31).

Making the Tough Choices

Think about it—you must decide daily what you will wear. Every day you are confronted with a heart issue. Will you put God at the center of your life when it comes to something as simple and practical as what you decide to wear? Will you seek to please Him? Will you think twice and choose clothes that honor God and speak well of Him? Will you, as one of the verses above says, choose to wear what is appropriate for a young man who professes to worship God?

Make it the desire of your heart to dress to impress God. Dress to catch the look of approval in His eyes. Dress to draw attention to your Savior, your godliness, and your good works so that your Father who is in heaven is glorified (Matthew 5:16). Choosing what you wear is not a small thing. No, it's a big deal! So make sure you're sending out the right message.

What will help you? First, know what the Bible says. Hopefully the verses shared in this chapter will guide you. Next, pray that you will want what God wants. Also, talk to your youth leader or an older teen or college guy or church leader you admire and respect. Ask his opinion. Then choose carefully what you wear. You can make a powerful statement by dressing in a fresh, pure, innocent style. Yes, you can wear clothes that are cool and fashionable and still follow God's guidelines. It's what's in your heart that counts. You need only to concern yourself with pleasing God, with following Him and His Word.

Guy to Guy

Jot down three evidences that Jason was not giving his clothing choices enough attention.

What could you now tell Jason about making better clothes choices?

Of all the verses shared in this chapter, which one meant the most to you that you could pass on to Jason, and why?

In what ways are you like Jason, and what new choices do you need to start making about your wardrobe?

Would You Like to Know More?
Check It Out

More important than what you choose to put on your body every day is making sure you choose to clothe yourself spiritually. What do these scriptures tell you to definitely include in your daily wardrobe, and why?

Ephesians 4:24—

Ephesians 6, verse 11—

Verse 13—

Verse 14—

Verse 15—

Verse 16—

Verse 17—

Colossians 3, verse 12—

Verse 14—

1 Peter 5:5—

Scan back through your answers and thoughts. Then circle or check several clothes choices you need to make a habit of.

God's Guidelines for Making Right Choices

- *Wear what fits the occasion*—"Be very careful, then, how you live—not as unwise but as wise" (Ephesians 5:15).

- *Wear what meets the approval of your parents*—"Children, obey your parents in the Lord, for this is right. 'Honor your father and mother'" (Ephesians 6:1-2).

- *Wear what doesn't attract attention to yourself*—"Do nothing out of selfish ambition or vain conceit, but in humility consider others better than yourselves. Each of you should look not only to your own interests, but also to the interests of others" (Philippians 2:3-4).

- *Wear your clothes to honor Christ*—"Whatever you do, whether in word or deed, do it all in the name of the Lord Jesus" (Colossians 3:17).

Silence Is Not Golden

*A man finds joy in giving an apt reply—
and how good is a timely word!*

—Proverbs 15:23

"J ason, did you hear your Uncle Ted's question?" Mom whispered.

"Question? What question?" Jason was completely focused on his new computer war game. And wow, he couldn't believe he was already on level three! *There are some really awesome weapons at this level,* he thought. But the irritated tone of his mother's voice had stirred Jason back to reality. "Sorry, Uncle Ted… what did you say?"

This wasn't an isolated incident. Jason loved to withdraw to his computer and video games, where he could be a superhero. Unfortunately, his frequent daydreams in fantasy worlds while at home and school had begun to take their toll on Jason's ability to communicate. Oh, he knew how to grunt a few appropriate words when confronted, like those he had just uttered to his uncle, with a little nudge from his mother. But to carry on an extended conversation or give a stand-up report in class? That was expecting too much of him. No way.

Poor Jason. If a cute girl said "Hi," about the best he could manage was a gulp. Whenever someone asked him, "What's up, dude?" his standard response was, "Hey, dude." Whenever Mom and Dad had someone over for dinner, the time at the table was pure agony. Because Jason never knew what to say, he usually sat and stared at his hands, wondering, *When is this ever going to be over?* And church? Well, Jason did okay with his guy friends, but he knew every way out of a room and was a master at avoiding talking to anyone.

Well, help is on the way for Jason, and for you too if you need a few pointers. Read on!

What Do I Want?

I would imagine this question has often been on your mind. Probably most family members and some others have asked you, at one time or another, about what you want for the future. I'm sure there are many things you can think of, and as time goes on you'll have more to add to the list. As you ponder how you would answer, here are some additional questions you can ask as you come up with answers to the question above.

- What do I truly want for my life?
- What do I want others to know about me, my thoughts, dreams, desires, knowledge, and experiences?
- What is required for me to do well in school?

- What must I do to get my parents to buy me that new computer game? No, make that a car!
- What is required for me to get the attention of a certain girl in my youth group?
- How would I convince a future boss that he should hire me?

And hopefully, one of the most important questions:

- What do I want people to know about Jesus?

Admittedly, some of your desires may have selfish motives behind them, but you may have others that are noble and worthy. The key to giving better answers on your "Here's what I want" list is having at least some ability to communicate. An ability to persuade. An ability to accurately share ideas and information. Unless you are able to speak effectively and talk with and to others, you may never see your desires and dreams become reality. Just about anything in life you might want will require that you ask for it. So, how good are you at persuasion? Persuading others is the ability to get others to agree with you, believe in something you say, or accept something you have heard, read, or thought. To get more positive responses, you need to develop an ability to speak and provide sound reasoning behind what you say.

Now this is where the choices you make can have an impact on your life. As we have said, every choice is important. Every choice gives direction, provides momentum, and has consequences, whether good or bad. The choice to make the effort to communicate is a willful decision. So start today and make the choice not only to communicate, but to do a better job of it—with your parents, peers, teachers, and adults in general.

Checking Out God's Word

Have you ever thought about why God gave us language? The answer is obvious isn't it—so that we can talk with each other, right? You are a unique person who has something to offer others, and others are unique as well and they have things to offer you. If you are persuasive enough, what you say can and should have a positive effect on others. And the reverse is true as well—it's possible for you to benefit from what others share with you.

That's exactly what God wanted for Moses when He spoke to Moses from a burning bush. God told Moses to take an important message to the children of Israel and to an oppressive king. Moses then tried to get out of doing that by giving God a series of excuses. But basically Moses was afraid to speak! You can read all about it in Exodus 3:10–4:11, but in a nutshell, this is sort of how the conversation went:

God speaks: "I am going to send you to the king of Egypt [Pharaoh] with a message to let My people go."

Moses' excuse #1: "Who am I? I'm a nobody!"

God didn't accept Moses' excuse, so…

Moses' excuse #2: "I don't know who is sending me"

God speaks: "I AM WHO I AM" (Exodus 3:14).

Moses' excuse #3: "What if the people will not believe me?"

God's promise: He will give Moses a sign to use when the people or Pharaoh question what God is asking of them through Moses—Moses' staff will turn into a snake.

Moses' excuse #4: "Please, Lord, I have never been much of a speaker. Send someone else!"

God's final word: "The LORD said to him, 'Who gave man his mouth? Who makes him deaf or mute? Who gives him sight or makes him blind? Is it not I, the LORD? Now go; I will help you speak and will teach you what to say'" (Exodus 4:11-12).

Note communication principle #1—*Speaking is a gift from God.*

The point is that God has given us our mouths and, as was the case with Moses, God expects us to use our mouths to serve Him. Now, His communication assignments to you will probably not be as dramatic as Moses'. But God still wants you to open your mouth and be His spokesman. And I'm sure you know the outcome of Moses' obedience: He became one of the most dynamic leaders of all time. And it all started when he was finally willing to open his mouth and speak for God.

Learning to Communicate

Isn't it encouraging to know that the great Moses had a bit of a problem with self-confidence? Before Moses heard from God at the burning bush, he had spent 40 years in the wilderness, where he didn't have to talk much at all. So Moses was definitely out of practice. Furthermore, he had no desire to speak to people. He just wanted to be left alone. (Is this sounding familiar?) But God had other plans for Moses. And guess what? He has other plans for you too. God made your mouth, and He wants you to speak up and talk to others. He wants you to communicate in a way that is necessary to do well in school, even if that means giving verbal reports. From this passage we learn...

Communication principle #2—*Speaking is a natural ability.*

But there's more. Moses was still lacking confidence, so God gave him a little help to get started:

> *Then the LORD's anger burned against Moses and he said, "What about your brother, Aaron the Levite? I know he can speak well. He is already on his way to meet you, and his heart will be glad when he sees you. You shall speak to him and put words in his mouth; I will help both of you speak and will teach you what to do"* (Exodus 4:14-15).

For a while Moses and Aaron, his brother, spoke to the people and to Pharaoh. But then something happened. Exodus 6:9 says, "Moses reported...to the Israelites, but they did not listen to him because of their discouragement and cruel bondage."

From this point onward, Moses did all the talking with the Israelites and to Pharaoh. As time progressed, Moses realized that he too could communicate. He began to understand that he didn't need the help of his brother. This brings us to...

Communication principle #3—*We learn to speak by speaking.*

So are you ready to become a better communicator? Here are some tips that will help. Notice that anyone can apply these tips.

So don't freak out. God is not asking you to join the debate team. He's only asking you to follow in Moses' footsteps and realize that speaking is natural and that you learn to speak by speaking.

Tips for Learning to Communicate

I know it's probably shaky ground to even think about speaking and giving a presentation and talking to people. I know that was once the case for me. But because of my job, I had to learn some basic communication skills. So I enrolled in an organization that teaches people like you and me how to communicate. Here are a few tips I learned—tips that still help me today.

1. Learn to Listen

Think back to our friend Jason. He had tuned out his uncle, who had asked him a question. And what was puzzling about Jason's actions was that Jason admired his Uncle Ted, a soldier in a special forces unit. Ted had traveled all over the world on secret missions and been involved in some pretty cool stuff. If Jason had stopped focusing on himself and made an effort to feel more comfortable with people, he could listen to his uncle talk and learn a lot about life and how to be successful. There was never any doubt that Uncle Ted was totally cool. He seemed to be larger than life and not only strong physically, but strong in character as well. To listen to someone is a sign of respect—whether it involves your parents, teachers, youth leaders, pastor...or uncle.

2. Learn to ask Questions.

Jason had a perfect opportunity to find out what he would need to do if he wanted to follow in his uncle's footsteps. Talk about adventure! Uncle Ted was just about everything Jason dreamed of being himself. Uncle Ted was living the life! Jason had already known his uncle was coming for a visit, so he had plenty of opportunity in advance to think of questions he could ask his uncle—questions such as, What kind of education would prepare him for admission into the Army? What training would he have to complete so he could qualify for this elite group of soldiers?

If Jason had turned his attention off of himself and his lack of comfort when he was with people and focused on Ted, and if Jason had chosen to just listen, observe, and learn, he would have known what questions to ask. Ted would have been more than happy to talk. In fact, he was even trying to start a conversation with Jason. Uncle Ted really liked his job and was proud of what he did. This brings up an important point about communications: It's not just talking to others, but it also involves letting others talk. But alas, Jason chose to withdraw into his computer game—into his comfort zone—and missed a perfect opportunity to get to know his uncle better and maybe have a life-changing experience.

3. Learn to Talk

As is the case with any other discipline, talking is a learned behavior. You don't become a good at sports or anything else without practice. The same is true about speaking. You learn by doing. As happened with Moses, the more you talk, the better and more comfortable you become with communicating.

Here's an idea for you. What about taking a speech class in school? You probably don't want to do this, but as we've just seen, you learn by doing. And what better way is there to learn than having someone teach and coach you on how to give presentations?

4. *Learn to Think Before You Talk*

Learning to communicate is vital. It's one of the most important choices you will ever make. But learning to talk more comes with the responsibility to speak in a serious and polite manner. Here are some biblical guidelines and cautions on how to speak and what to say. You can take notes now, or later.

> *He who guards his lips guards his life, but he who speaks rashly will come to ruin* (Proverbs 13:3).

> *Words from a wise man's mouth are gracious, but a fool is consumed by his own lips. At the beginning his words are folly; at the end they are wicked madness* (Ecclesiastes 10:12-13).

> *Nor should there be obscenity, foolish talk or coarse joking, which are out of place, but rather thanksgiving* (Ephesians 5:4).

> *A fool has no pleasure in understanding, but delights in airing his own opinions* (Proverbs 18:2).

He who answers before listening—that is his folly and his shame (verse 13).

5. Learn the Importance of Two-way Communication

As I said earlier, your goal is to get the other person talking. Neither you nor others want to listen to you do all the talking. Communication involves both giving and receiving information. Notice how, as a boy of 12, Jesus was communicating in Luke 2:46. Also notice who He was communicating with:

After three days they [His parents] found him in the temple courts, sitting among the teachers, listening to them and asking them questions.

6. Learn the Art of Nonverbal Communication

By this I mean paying attention to what your actions communicate to the people around you. For example:

- When you fail to respond to questions, even in your silence you communicate.
- When you turn your back or pretend to be occupied with something else, you communicate.
- When you choose not to look at a person who is asking you a question, you communicate.
- When you are asked a question and you answer with

a grunt or a shrug of your shoulders or even a "Yep" or "Nope," you communicate.

Remember—communicating is more than just speaking. Your nonverbal actions say a lot to others.

7. Learn the Importance of Telling the Truth

Even the most silent person must open his mouth when asked a direct question like, "Did you do this or not?" Now comes the moment when you must open your mouth and say something. But suppose telling the truth would get you in trouble—then what do you do?

To avoid getting in trouble, you might find yourself wanting to tell a lie or tell a half-truth, which is the same as telling a lie. Or you might find yourself tempted to lie, and then blame your lying on someone else by saying, "The devil made me do it!" But you know that's not what Jesus wants. As a Christian, by a choice of your will and with the help of the Holy Spirit, you can choose to follow the command of Ephesians 4:25:

> *Each of you must put off falsehood and speak truthfully to his neighbor, for we are all members of one body.*

God has given you and me a very clear picture of truth in His Son and in His Word. When you disregard the truth and make a decision based on pressure and fear of what others might say or do, you compromise all that you say you believe.

Do you want to know how you can honor God and glorify His Son? Allow the truth that dwells in you to control your speech and your actions. Choose to speak the truth no matter what the consequences.

Making the Tough Choices

For most guys, communication is not easy. Often you would rather keep your mouth shut and be safe, rather than look awkward or have others think you are a fool. But you must choose to come out of your comfort zone. Choosing to keep silent is a selfish act. When you do that you are saying , "I'm not interested in you or what you have to say. And I don't want you to know anything about me."

Making the choice to communicate is not easy. But as you make an effort to talk, you will make friends more easily, learn exciting things about people, and have opportunities to share with others some of what God has given you. And, a couple added bonuses are that you will be happy and others will be blessed! "A [young] man finds joy in giving an apt reply—and how good is a timely word!" (Proverbs 15:23).

Guy to Guy

Jot down several things Jason did wrong during his time with his uncle.

What could you tell Jason to do differently when he's around others?

Of all the verses shared in this chapter, which one meant the most to you, and why?

In what ways are you like Jason? What new choices will you start making about how you communicate?

Would You Like to Know More?
Check It Out

What do these verses teach you about your speech?

Proverbs 4:24—

Proverbs 6:12—

Proverbs 6:16-19 (list what these verses say regarding speech)—

Ephesians 4:15—

Ephesians 4:29—

Colossians 3:8-9 (list what should not be a part of your speech)—

1 Peter 2:21-22—

God's Guidelines for Making Right Choices

- *Don't interrupt others; wait patiently until they finish.* "[There is] a time to be silent and a time to speak" (Ecclesiastes 3:7).

- *Don't belittle or put down another person.* "Instead, speaking the truth in love, we will in all things grow up into him who is the Head, that is, Christ" (Ephesians 4:15).

- *Don't be critical of another person.* "Do not let any unwholesome talk come out of your mouths, but only what is helpful for building others up according to their needs, that it may benefit those who listen" (Ephesians 4:29).

- *Do have a pleasant attitude as you speak.* "The wise in heart are called discerning, and pleasant words promote instruction" (Proverbs 16:21).

- *Do be ready to speak about Jesus.* "Let your conversation be always full of grace, seasoned with salt, so that you may know how to answer everyone" (Colossians 4:6).

- *Don't speak in anger.* "Everyone should be quick to listen, slow to speak and slow to become angry" (James 1:19).

- *Remember that how you say what you say is important.* "A gentle answer turns away wrath, but a harsh word stirs up anger" (Proverbs 15:1).

The Road to Success

Jesus grew in wisdom and stature,
and in favor with God and men.

—LUKE 2:52

As the bus turned the corner and entered the school campus, Jason's day—from his perspective—was about to sink to its lowest point. Nothing could make it any worse. The time had come for the part of the day he dreaded most—school.

Ugh! School is such a drag. I know I have to go to school, but... why? Jason thought. *I don't want or plan to go to college. So what's the big deal? And so what if I goof off once in a while in class and do below-average work? None of that will matter anymore when I'm done with school.*

Jason dared to dream. *If I can just scrape through and graduate, then everything will be great. I'll find a good-paying job, get my own apartment, buy a great gaming system, and spend my free time hanging out with friends. Who needs school anyway?*

The door of the bus opened, and everyone filed out. Eventually Jason was the only one left. As had happened on other days, the bus driver, Mrs Bradford, said, "Jason, you know you can't stay here. Go on! Get out and take your medicine."

And that's exactly how Jason felt—as if school were a bitter medicine. *Somehow,* he reasoned to himself, *I've got to endure this awful school thing.* Then after a brief pause he thought, *Well, look on the bright side—I hang out with a bunch of other guys who feel the same way I do.*

As Jason made his way to his first class, he was somewhat comforted as he looked around and sighed, "Misery loves company!"

A Dose of Reality

Jason's attitude toward school reminds me of the young men and women of my hometown who also struggled and wondered whether school was all that important. In our town was a large manufacturing plant that hired many of the local residents. Every year, a large number of the high school graduates would go to work for the plant or for a business that was in some way connected with the plant. All through school most of my friends counted on getting one of these jobs, which would keep them in the local area. And while the jobs paid well, they didn't require more than a basic education.

I too was heading in the same direction—just going through the motions, not really that interested in school. But that began to change when a local pharmacist took an interest in me and hired me to work in his pharmacy. After a while I turned my focus from settling for a job at the local plant and started to concentrate on my studies so I could become a pharmacist.

The sad part of this story is that the local plant closed down the year after I graduated from high school. Many of my school friends, as well as about half the people in the town, were suddenly out of a job. And because most of the workers and young people had not planned ahead and made an effort to do well in school, their prospects for the future were dashed on the rocks of reality.

Checking Out God's Word

God created you and me with a mind. And amazingly, our minds are more complex than any computer. What's more, God expects you to train and develop your mind. Look at these verses and think about how they might apply to you and learning. If you want, you can also write down your thoughts.

> *Listen, my sons, to a father's instruction; pay attention and gain understanding. I give you sound learning, so do not forsake my teaching* (Proverbs 4:1-3).

> *Get wisdom, get understanding... Wisdom is supreme; therefore get wisdom* (Proverbs 4:5,7).

Whatever you do, work at it with all your heart, as
working for the Lord, not for men (Colossians 3:23).

Maybe you haven't thought much about it, but Jesus had to
go to school and get an education and grow in knowledge (Luke
2:42,46-47). For instance, we read that "Jesus grew in wisdom
and stature, and in favor with God and men" (Luke 2:52).

The Importance of Today

Now, before you give up on me because you don't like school,
realize I'm not encouraging you to spend the next ten years of
your life with your head in a book. Rather, I simply want to point
out the importance of learning what you can just for today. The
habits and disciplines you acquire one day at a time over the next
few years will lay the foundation for the rest of your life. You can
choose today—and every day—to make an effort to learn and
grow in your knowledge of both the things of God and the information and skills that will enable you to make a living and
enjoy life.

You never know what the future holds. It's hard to know
right now exactly what you will need in the way of education
and training. So make sure you take advantage of any and every
opportunity you have to learn and grow. And do this just one
day at a time. Think about the importance of the choices you
make today:

- Today's *good choices* will give you the freedom to choose
  greater opportunities tomorrow.

- Today's *good habits* will give you greater discipline for choosing to accept greater challenges tomorrow.
- Today's *good attitudes* will equip you to choose to run the greater race and for winning the greater prize tomorrow (1 Corinthians 9:24).

Becoming a Learner for Life

My wife once told me of the words on the tombstone of a well-known scientist: "He Died Learning." That made a great impression on me. Since then, I have tried to follow this man's example. And I hope this will become your motto as well. Unfortunately, there are guys (like our friend Jason) whose motto is "I would rather die than learn." They dislike school and can't wait for graduation so they can get on with "real life." And like Jason they go through the motions, exerting only the minimum effort necessary to get by. Sadly, when tomorrow arrives, they will wake up and discover that they have very limited career options because they didn't develop the skills or acquire the disciplines that were needed for the challenges of the future.

Now maybe you're thinking, *Yeah, I get it. But I'm not a very good student. I try, but I never seem to do very well.* Well, friend, there is hope. You need to realize there are two kinds of learning—formal and informal. Formal learning takes place with the help of textbooks and, in most cases, within the four walls of a classroom. You don't have much choice about this type of learning. It's what the school system dictates (or, if you are homeschooled, it's what your parents expect). But even if you struggle, it is still necessary for you to try your best because formal learning is what gives you the foundation and discipline for all the learning that you can choose to gain outside the classroom.

That's the informal learning! This type of learning has to do with your personal desires and dreams. Informal learning provides you with limitless choices you can make every day. It's an ongoing activity that will last your entire lifetime.

Remember what I said earlier about a pharmacist who took an interest in me? While I worked at his pharmacy, informally I learned about medicine, medications, chemistry, and retail sales. The pharmacist was a willing teacher, and I was a willing student. That informal learning shaped my future for many years to come. But it was my formal learning that made it possible for me to pursue the informal learning.

So don't panic when someone says you need to get an education. There are lots of ways to learn, as you can see below:

- *Learning is an attitude*—it involves heart and head.

- *Learning is progressive*—it builds upon itself.

- *Learning is not dependent on your IQ*—it depends on your desire.

- *Learning has no boundaries or limits*—except those you place on yourself.

- *Learning does not require social status or money*—it's free to anyone with a desire to expand his or her knowledge.

- *Learning has its own rewards*—its prizes are unlimited.

- *Learning has as ultimate priority*—you want to know more about Jesus Christ and how to live His way (2 Peter 3:18).

How to Enjoy a Life of Learning

Are you wondering, *Yes, but how?* Here are a few simple suggestions for making learning fun and exciting as you continue to learn for a lifetime:

Become a zealous reader. Reading is the window to all learning. Not everyone is like Uncle Ted. Few people get to adventure their way around the world. But reading exposes you to the entire globe and to the knowledge and experiences of others. Say, for instance, you read one of my books, like this one. The information you read in a few hours or days took me many years to learn, apply, and formulate into a book. Now, in a very short time, you know most of what I know from a lifetime of studying and practicing the subject of "making choices." How's that for learning from others?

One word of caution: Be selective in your reading. Comic books are easy to read and provide lots of diversion, but they are just stories which may or may not be helpful and edifying. Choose books that will build you up. Books that will encourage and stretch and challenge and inspire you. Books that will teach and train you. That doesn't mean you don't read a comic every now and then. But you only have so much time, so choose wisely! After all, when it comes to applying for a job, it won't matter how many comic books you have in your collection or whether you know exactly how many different types of Spider Man comics have been produced. A prospective employer won't be impressed with your knowledge about comic books.

And don't forget—the first book you want to read and read again and again is the Bible. Read it a little at a time from cover to cover, over and over, for the rest of your life.

Become a guy who asks questions. Everyone has something to teach you. Everyone is an expert on something. Find out what that something is, and learn from these people. View every person as a teacher—starting with your parents! Is there someone who is doing something you would like to learn about? For instance, do you like playing games on a computer? Well, find someone who knows how to program and develop gaming programs. Contact him. Get together. Ask your questions. See if you can follow him around for a while to see what it is he does. How did he get his training? What would you have to do to acquire similar skills? Asking questions can help prepare you for your own future.

Be aware of the actions of others. Look around you. Who in your school or at church is acting in a responsible way? And who is acting irresponsibly, always in trouble, and getting attention for the wrong reasons? Who seems to have their act together, and who seems to be a mess? Who seems to be living a godly life, and who is saying and doing things that go against what you know and believe? Who seems to be moving in the direction you want to go? Observe both the good and bad. Take note of both. Then copy the good actions of others and avoid the bad ones.

Be learning from the experiences of others. Obviously adults have a few more life experiences than a teen boy. So, once again, look around at those who have gained experience that would give you insight for your own life and future and the things you want to do.

Let's say you're interested in missionary work. The next time a missionary visits your church, find an opportunity to ask him about his experiences on the mission field. Or maybe you are interested in the medical profession. Talk to a doctor or nurse or pharmacist about their experiences. Or what boy hasn't dreamed of becoming a policeman? Perhaps you have one or more right in your own church you could talk to and learn from.

And once again, back to reading. As you read, you can learn from the biographies of the great men and women of history. What were their experiences? Were they a business tycoon? A war hero? A dynamic preacher? An inventor? An astronaut? As you read about such people, pay attention to their experiences as a leader, a husband, a father, and a friend. Reading is a quick and enriching way to learn from people's successes…and to learn about how to avoid the mistakes they made.

And, I repeat, don't forget your Bible. The Bible is the best of all books for learning from the experience of others. And it was written by God Himself!

Making the Tough Choices

I pray that you will never stop learning. Learning will develop your most important resource—your life! A life that God desires to use for His glory. You've seen this verse before in this book, and it applies here to your learning as well: "Whether you eat or drink or whatever you do, do it all for the glory of God" (1 Corinthians 10:31). And to ensure that you are always learning, ask yourself the following question each day:

- What new thing can I learn *today*?
- Who can I learn from *today*?
- How can I be challenged in some aspect of my life *today*?
- How can I become more Christlike *today*?

Guy to Guy

Jot down three wrong assumptions that Jason had about learning and his future.

What could you tell Jason about the importance of learning in preparation for the future?

Of all the verses shared in this chapter, which one meant the most to you that you could pass on to Jason?

In what ways are you like Jason, and what new choices do you need to start making?

Would You Like to Know More?
Check It Out

Here are three people who were significantly used by God. Note the common theme in all their lives.

Daniel was just a teen when he was carried off to captivity in Babylon. In spite of his difficult situation, he became a man who was greatly used of God. How did he become prepared for the future (Daniel 1:4)?

How well did Daniel and his three friends prepare themselves (Daniel 1:19-20)?

How much responsibility was Daniel given because of his abilities (Daniel 2:48)?

What influence did Daniel have with the king (Daniel 2:49)?

Jesus was unique because He was God in human flesh, but He still developed in key areas just like other humans. List these four key areas and circle how "learning" is described in Luke 2:52.

—

—

—

—

What insights about your own development can you learn from this verse? And where do you need to put more effort?

Paul was a great man who wrote 13 of the books in the New Testament. What do you learn about his preparation for the future, according to Acts 22:3?

How else was Paul prepared for a life of usefulness, according to Galatians 1:11-12? (Just a note: Our "revelation" today comes as we read and study God's written revelation, the Bible.)

Realize that as you allow God to work through your life, you can contribute mightily to the good of others. But usefulness doesn't come automatically. How should you view preparing for your unknown future?

Do's and Don'ts for Being a Better Student

- *Do your homework each day.* Do it while you're fresh. You'll feel great when you finish and it will be a big burden off your back.

- *Do reward yourself for getting your homework done.* After you finish your schoolwork, it's okay to play that video game, watch some TV, read a good book, call a friend, or just kick back! (That is, if it's okay with Dad and Mom.)

- *Do your projects early, not the night before they are due.* Don't wait until the last minute. Working in advance allows you time to also have fun, and you'll have the assurance of not hurting your schoolwork and grades.

- *Do keep your homework assignments close by at all times.* You would be surprised how many free minutes there are each day—even while you're at school—that could be used to finish your homework or work ahead. How great to have finished your assignments before leaving school each day!

- *Do ask for help.* Teachers don't mind when their students ask for information. In fact, teachers love it when students show a desire to learn and do better in class. If you are unsure of an assignment or when the next test is scheduled, ask the teacher or another student for the information. (And don't forget to write it down so you don't have to ask again.)

- *Do take notes in class.* Taking notes will keep you alert and focused regardless of how boring the subject is. Remember, even the boring parts of your teacher's lectures will probably be on the next exam. Taking notes is a shortcut to knowledge and an excellent habit.

- *Don't wait until the last minute to study for an exam.* Spread your study time over a period of several days in advance of the test. Cramming the night before may get you by in an emergency, but studying some each day over a period of several days will help you know the material better and make it easier to remember in the future.

- *Don't be late for school or class.* Showing up on time is a key to success. So develop a habit of showing up on time or even early. That little bit of discipline will take you far in this world.

- *Don't cheat.* It goes against God's Word and His plan for you as a Christian. Cheating is a fool's definition of success. You're better than that. No grade is worth dishonoring God.

- *Don't forget to pray.* You'll be surprised how much difference prayer makes when you do it each morning. Pray that you'll be a better student, pay more attention at school, and be more diligent in completing your school assignments.

A Word About Learning from Socrates

A young man came to the great philosopher and teacher Socrates one day and said, in substance: "Socrates, I have come 1500 miles to gain wisdom and learning. I want to learn, so I came to you." Socrates said, "Come, follow me." He led the way to the seashore. They waded out into the water until they were up to their waists. Then Socrates seized his companion and forced his head under the water. In spite of the young man's struggle, Socrates held him under.

Finally, when most of his resistance was gone, Socrates pulled him out on the shore and then returned to the marketplace. When the visitor regained his strength, he went back to Socrates to ask why the teacher had done such a terrible thing.

Socrates said to him, "When you were under the water, what was the one thing you wanted more than anything else?"

"I wanted air."

Then Socrates said, "When you want knowledge and understanding as badly as you wanted air, you won't have to ask anyone to give it to you."[1]

God's Guidelines for
Making Right Choices

- *Make God your Number One priority*—"Seek first his kingdom and his righteousness, and all these things will be given to you as well" (Matthew 6:33).

- *Remember why you do your best*—"Whatever you do, work at it with all your heart, as working for the Lord, not for men, since you know that you will receive an inheritance from the Lord as a reward. It is the Lord Christ you are serving" (Colossians 3:23-24).

- *Focus on what's right in front of you*—"A discerning man keeps wisdom in view, but a fool's eyes wander to the ends of the earth" (Proverbs 17:24).

- *Keep moving forward*—"Brothers, I do not consider myself yet to have taken hold of it. But one thing I do: Forgetting what is behind and straining toward what is ahead, I press on toward the goal to win the prize for which God has called me heavenward in Christ Jesus" (Philippians 3:13-14).

- *Work hard at whatever you do*—"Whatever your hand finds to do, do it with all your might, for in the grave, where you are going, there is neither working nor planning nor knowledge nor wisdom" (Ecclesiastes 9:10).

Hanging Out

*Encourage one another and
build each other up.*

—1 THESSALONIANS 5:11

When we last looked at Jason, he was slowly making his way through the crowded school hall to his locker before the start of his first class. Upon arriving at his locker, Jason sees Isaac, whose locker is next to his. Jason has known Isaac for years. For a while they were part of the same youth group at church.

Isaac and Jason had been tight for as long as Jason could remember. But this year something had happened. He and Isaac seemed to be drifting apart. You see, Jason had decided to branch out in his friendships. Isaac and the other church kids just weren't that popular and always seemed out of place. In Jason's opinion, they dressed a little weird and even acted a little weird. That's why Jason had changed the kind of clothes he was now wearing. Matt, one of Jason's new friends, says Isaac is wimpy. He even calls Isaac and Jason's other church friends "religious weirdos."

Jason gives Isaac a quick smile as they greet. Then, just as quickly, Jason grabs his books to dash. "See ya at youth group tonight?" Isaac calls out as Jason heads for class.

Jason likes Isaac and the others from church and he has a good time when he's with them, away from his new friends and away from school. In fact, he wishes he could be as strong as Isaac when it comes to living boldly for Jesus, but he doesn't like standing out or being seen as different. Boy, is Jason ever in turmoil! He wants to be liked, especially by the "in crowd" at school.

And speaking of the "in crowd," here comes Matt. "Hey Jason, that's an awesome shirt! I don't think I've seen it before. Dude, we'll make you one of us yet!" Jason was both pleased and sick, wondering, *How am I going to resolve this conflict?*

Being a Friend

You may be one of those guys who has never met a stranger. Maybe you can talk to just about anyone and make friends easily. Or maybe, like Jason, you have a longtime childhood friend like Isaac, and the two of you are inseparable. But for a lot of guys it's not easy to find a good friend. So whether you have many friends or a few, I'm sure you will agree that friendship is a two-way street. If you want a good friend, you have to be a good friend. So for you and me (two guys who have to work at making friends), we need to begin our discussion of friendships by talking about what makes a guy a good friend.

Checking Out God's Word

In the Bible, God gives guidelines on how to be a good friend. As you read through these verses, think about your friendships and determine whether you are trying to be the kind of friend God describes here. Also, be thinking of what a friend—a real friend—does and does not do.

He who covers over an offense promotes love, but whoever repeats the matter separates close friends (Proverbs 17:9).

A friend loves at all times, and a brother is born for adversity (Proverbs 17:17).

A man of many companions may come to ruin, but there is a friend who sticks closer than a brother (Proverbs 18:24).

Wounds from a friend can be trusted, but an enemy multiplies kisses (Proverbs 27:6).

Do not forsake your friend (Proverbs 27:10).

As iron sharpens iron, so one man sharpens another (Proverbs 27:17).

Being the Right Kind of Friend

How can you choose friends that last? As I said earlier, developing the right friendships starts with you—you need to be the right kind of friend. Here are some choices you'll need to make if you want to be a top-notch friend. If you make these choices, the right kind of guys will be standing in line to be your friend.

1. Choose to Be Growing Spiritually

This is a key choice you must make in each and every area of your life, and friendships are no different. If you desire to grow spiritually and get closer to God, you won't settle for anything less than a friend who also shares your passion for God. And where will you find this kind of person? Here's a hint—you'll usually find these guy-friends at church or in a Christian youth group.

2. Choose to Be Yourself

Don't try to impress others by saying and doing things you think will make them like you. And this goes double if your actions would be contrary to God's Word in any way. Remember, you are looking for a friend who isn't phony—who isn't pretending to be one person when he's really someone else. So choose to be what God wants you to be. Be a young man who honors the Lord. You probably won't be the most popular guy at school, but you will be *you*. You will be genuine. And you'll be free of the inner conflict Jason is experiencing. When you are comfortable with who you are, then others will also feel comfortable when they're around you. They might not share your beliefs, but they will respect you for what you stand for. So just be yourself. Be friendly and helpful to everyone, but don't hesitate to be bold and put God first. Try your best to live His way. And hang out with others who put God first. As you do so, God will bring along like-minded people to be your friends.

3. Choose to Be Loyal

Have you ever heard of a fair-weather friend? I'm sure you know exactly what this means. It's a so-called friend who bails as soon as something goes wrong. They're great friends as long as things don't get complicated. Usually the friendship is one-way. As long as you do things the other person's way, everything is fine. But the minute you do something he doesn't like, try being your real self, or have a serious need in your life, that "friend" fades away into the night, wanting nothing to do with you.

Loyalty is essential in any friendship. Therefore, you must become a loyal friend yourself. In the Bible, David and Jonathan's friendship was characterized by loyalty even in the midst of severe adversity. (You can read about their friendship in 1 Samuel 20:14-18.)

How loyal are you as a friend? Are you "a friend who sticks closer than a brother" (Proverbs 18:24)? Loyalty in others starts with you being loyal.

4. Choose to Be Honest

Trust is essential in any relationship. If you want to have friends who are honest with you, then (you guessed it) you must be honest with them. Honesty is one of the benefits of a true friendship. The Bible puts it this way: "Wounds from a friend can be trusted...and the pleasantness of one's friend springs from his earnest counsel" (Proverbs 27:6,9). You and a true friend should be committed to pulling each other toward God's goals and standards for young men who want to live for God.

5. Choose to Encourage

Have you ever thought about how easy it is to tell people all the things they're doing "wrong" (at least from your perspective)? They're wearing the wrong clothes or acting the wrong way. It's much better to make it a habit to pick out actions and attitudes that are right about others.

What is the best way to be an encourager? Let's go back to the two guy-friends, David and Jonathan, for just a moment. Their friendship was based on their mutual love for God. When David was marked for murder by Jonathan's father, King Saul, "Jonathan went to David…and helped him find strength in God" (1 Samuel 23:16).

The Bible says that we are to "encourage one another and build each other up" (1 Thessalonians 5:11). The best way to encourage a friend is to help him find strength in God through the Scriptures. You can also take time to pray for each other. And don't forget to give compliments. Be specific with your praise. Say something specific that you appreciate about your friend, something you see in his conduct or admire in his character. Make it a goal to build up other people instead of tearing them down. Your friends are a reflection of you. They are what you are becoming. (Think about *that* for a minute or two!)

6. *Choose to Work At Friendships*

Good friendships, the right kind of friendships, don't just happen overnight. You have to make a willful choice about keeping and growing these kinds of friendships. Don't do what Jason did. He was making a choice to leave a good friend behind for a questionable friend. Friendship takes time and effort. So sit together at lunch. Call, e-mail, or text. Hang out together. When the apostle Paul wrote to his friends in Philippi, he said, "I have you in my heart" (Philippians 1:7). Do you have a best friend? What can you do today to strengthen that friendship?

Finding a Friend

Now for the hardest thing to do—finding good friends! It's not easy. And it may take some time. So be patient. Put this on your prayer list. In the meantime, remember:

You have a friend in Jesus. Realize that if you are a Christian you already have the greatest friend ever—a forever friend. You have a friend in Jesus, God's own Son. Jesus has chosen you to belong to Him and be His friend. Jesus said to His disciples, "You are my friends…I have called you friends" (John 15:14-15). And He's saying the same to you. With Jesus as your friend, you really don't need anyone else. But God also provides others friends to provide companionship with you.

You have friends in your parents. Now, before you tune me out, realize that there is nothing weird about having your mom and dad as your best friends. They are God's gifts to you. Hopefully, even if it's not clear right now, you will understand that no one loves you more or cares for your best interests more than your parents do. Ask God to help you develop a level of friendship with your parents. Trust me, in later years you'll discover what I'm telling you is true.

You also have friends in your brothers and sisters. You are probably thinking, *Being friends with my goofy brother? No way…ever!* Or *Friends with my little sister? You've got to be kidding!* But realize that as time goes on, your friends will come and go. You might stay in touch with some, but most of your friends will move on. But your family will always be there, especially if you build and maintain friendships with them. And be encouraged! Your brother won't always be goofy, and your sister won't always be a brat.

Checking Out God's Word

The Bible is very clear and specific when it tells you the kind of person to look for in a friend…and what kind to avoid! Here's "God's List of People to Reject as Friends." As you read through these verses, notice what is said about the speech, character, and conduct of those who are not to be your friends and the dangerous effect they can have on you.

> *He who walks with the wise grows wise, but a companion of fools suffers harm* (Proverbs 13:20).

> *Do not make friends with a hot-tempered man, do not associate with one easily angered* (Proverbs 22:24).

> *You must not associate with anyone who calls himself a brother [a Christian] but is sexually immoral or greedy, an idolater or slanderer, a drunkard or a swindler* (1 Corinthians 5:11).

> *Do not be yoked together with unbelievers. For what do righteousness and wickedness have in common? Or what fellowship can light have with darkness?…What does a believer have in common with an unbeliever?* (2 Corinthians 6:14-15).

> *Do not be mislead: "Bad company corrupts good character"* (1 Corinthians 15:33).

Making the Tough Choices

There's no question that how you go about choosing friends and friendships is a crucial part of your life. Friends are one of the means God uses to encourage, teach, train, and mature you. It's been said that there are three kinds of people in your life—

those who pull you down (away from Jesus),
those who pull you along (in the direction of Jesus), and
those who pull you up (toward Jesus).

Obviously you should want to avoid those who pull you down. "Bad company" really does corrupt good character. So this leaves only those who pull you along and those who pull you up as candidates for real friendships. Therefore, it goes without saying, your best friends should be Christians, the kind of friends who will pull you along and up toward Christlikeness. Your best friends should be strong, like-minded believers who help you to think your best thoughts, do your most honorable deeds, and be your finest self.

As you go about the business of choosing friends…

- *Start with yourself.* Develop the qualities you desire in a friend. Be the kind of person who pulls others along and up toward God. Remember, like attracts like. What you are, you will attract.

- *Set the highest standards possible*—those we've been discussing from the Bible. Remember, it's better to have no friends than to have the wrong friends!

- *Select your friends wisely.* Remember that you are known by the company you keep.

Guy to Guy

Jot down three wrong assumptions that Jason had about friends, both old and new.

What could you tell Jason about the importance of being careful about his friendships?

Of all the verses shared in this chapter, which one meant the most to you that you could pass on to Jason?

In what ways are you like Jason, and what new choices do you need to start making?

Would You Like to Know More?
Check It Out

You've looked at the young Daniel before, but look again with friendships in mind. Write out the names of his three friends (Daniel 1:6-7).

What did these youths have in common (verses 3-6)?

Read Daniel 1:12-20. What situation did Daniel and his three friends have to endure together (verses 12-14)?

How did their time of testing turn out (verses 15-20)?

What other element do you find in their friendship in Daniel 2:16-18?

What impresses you most about the friendship that existed among these four young men?

Read 1 Samuel 18:1-4. Jonathan was the son of King Saul, whom David served. What do you learn about Jonathan and David's friendship in...

verse 1?—

verse 3?—

verse 4?—

And in 1 Samuel 23:16?—

What impresses you most about the friendship that existed between these two young men?

What do you learn about friends and friendship in...

James 2:23?—

James 4:4—

Thought question: Who are you a friend of?

God's Guidelines for Making Right Choices

- *Make friends who are real.* "A man of many companions may come to ruin, but there is a friend who sticks closer than a brother" (Proverbs 18:24).

- *Make friends who are faithful.* "A friend loves at all times, and a brother is born for adversity" (Proverbs 17:17).

- *Make friends who will hold you accountable.* "As iron sharpens iron, so one man sharpens another" (Proverbs 27:17).

- *Make friends with those who will encourage your growth.* "Therefore, my dear friends, as you have always obeyed—not only in my presence, but now much more in my absence—continue to work out your salvation with fear and trembling" (Philippians 2:12).

- *Make friends with like-minded guys.* "Flee the evil desires of youth, and pursue righteousness, faith, love and peace, along with those who call on the Lord out of a pure heart" (2 Timothy 2:22).

● ● ● ● ● ●

What About Girls?

Pursue righteousness, faith,
love and peace, along with those
who call on the Lord out of a pure heart.

—2 Timothy 2:22

Speaking of friends…here comes Carmen. As Jason stands at his locker fumbling through the massive mess of papers in search of his English class notes, he sees Carmen walking down the hall. Carmen is Jason's chemistry lab partner, and he believes he may just have a crush on her!

For the record, Jason and Carmen are not an item. True, she and Jason have gone out in the same group on several occasions. And, of course, they have spent some time together on science projects. Jason has even been to Carmen's house several times, and Carmen had come to Jason's house once when they had to work on their science fair project. Jason's parents liked Carmen.

They especially liked that she was polite, courteous, and well-mannered. But they also reminded Jason that, even with all her good qualities, there is one thing missing, the most important thing of all: Carmen was not a Christian.

But Jason really likes Carmen. And he can hardly believe it, but she seems to like him too! So Jason has tried to put aside his parents' concerns, thinking, *Carmen's a great girl. So what's the big deal about a difference or absence of religious beliefs?* Besides, Jason just knew that if their friendship turned into a relationship, true love would transcend all barriers. He even thought that if he and Carmen were closer, he could tell her about Jesus and maybe influence her positively about becoming a Christian. Then things would be different! And then Jason's parents would stop warning him to be cautious.

A Word About Girls

In the last chapter we talked about friends and friendships. You might have read that chapter thinking, *But what about girlfriends?* Well, we're about to answer that question. So what do we need to know about relationships with girls? Let's face it: You're around girls all day—at school, at church, and out in public. So it's important to know how to interact with them. Yet you have to approach boy-girl relationships in an entirely different way than you do friendships with guys. Yes, you should be friendly to everyone. But you should also be very cautious and take special care when it comes to friendships with girls. Here are five guidelines for making right choices:

1. *Beware of being too chummy.* Yes, be nice. But keep your friendship strictly "professional" even if the girl is your lab

partner at school or is involved in the same after-school study group or activity as you. Getting too close and acting too friendly may send out a wrong message. It could mislead a girl about your level of interest in her. And, as in Jason's case, the closer you get to a girl, the more influenced you are by your feelings toward her…which can easily lead to trouble!

2. *Beware of being too complimentary.* Another way to inadvertently send out the wrong message is to tell girls in general they are cute, or you like their clothes, hair, etc. Again, you should be nice. But flattery can also send a message that you never meant to send—that you are interested in a closer relationship—a boyfriend/girlfriend relationship, or that you are interested in them sexually. Here's a thought: If you really want to give a compliment, don't make it a physical compliment. Instead, mention a girl's character. For example, you could say, "I noticed how you helped Sheila pick up her books. That was nice."

3. *Beware of girls whose speech is questionable.* Here's one of the Bible's guidelines for girls: They are to have "a gentle and quiet spirit" (1 Peter 3:4). This means they don't run off at the mouth, that they aren't loud and boisterous. Also, you want to keep your distance from girls whose mouths are filled with "unwholesome talk…slander…malice…and filthy language" (Ephesians 4:29,31; Colossians 3:8). Do they use words that are dirty or have sexual meanings? God wants your friends, whether boys or girls, to be pure in speech as well as in body and mind.

4. *Beware of girls who dress inappropriately.* God expects Christians to hold the line when it comes to modesty and purity (1 Timothy 2:9). And He expects you, as a Christian, to hold the highest standards for yourself, your friends, and with girls. A sure giveaway of the inner qualities of a girl is seen in her choice of the clothes she wears. Avoid girls who see no problem with

wearing revealing clothes, who dress to draw attention to themselves, and especially from boys.

5. *Beware of getting too close to girls who are not Christians.* This is the most important guideline for you to follow when it comes to girls, friendships, dating, etc. Let's face it—when it comes to a boy-girl friendship, there is usually a progression: A friend becomes a girlfriend. And if the relationship continues to progress, the logical endpoint for a moral and honorable Christian young man like yourself is marriage, right? I know it's a shock to think about this now, and I'm guessing you are not thinking that far ahead, but it can't be anything else, unless you and the girl's purity are compromised. Right? So, if this is the eventual outcome of a dating relationship, make sure it starts with a Christian girl. The Bible is very clear about relationships with unbelievers. Just read 2 Corinthians 6:14—notice the big "do not" and the reasons why.

> *Do not be yoked together with unbelievers. For what do righteousness and wickedness have in common? Or what fellowship can light have with darkness?*

Checking Out God's Word

Boy-girl relationships have the potential to come with a high emotional price tag. If such relationships are not handled God's way, you can make mistakes that hurt both you and the girl—even mistakes that last a lifetime. The best way to prevent painful emotions and experiences—and regrets—is to set biblical standards for the kind of girl you would consider as a friend.

We've already seen the Number One qualification here: She must be a Christian. Beyond that, you need to follow the standards that God has set in His Word.

In the Bible you'll find a great role model of the kind of qualities a girl ought to have if you are thinking in terms of a friendship possibly turning into a dating relationship. This role model is found in Proverbs 31:10-31. In fact, this advice comes from the mother of a young king—she tells him the kind of woman he should look for, and she describes this woman's qualities—not her looks!—in detail. Whatever your age, and regardless of whether or not you are even interested in girls, take note of this list. Having a pen in your hand wouldn't hurt, and can only help as you read and note your observations.

> She is a woman of character—*The sayings of King Lemuel—an oracle his mother taught him...A wife of noble character who can find? She is worth far more than rubies* (Proverbs 31:1,10).

> She is faithful and trustworthy—*Her husband has full confidence in her and lacks nothing of value* (verse 11).

> She supports and encourages—*She brings him good, not harm, all the days of her life* (verse 12).

> She is selfless and generous—*She opens her arms to the poor and extends her hands to the needy* (verse 20).

> She is an excellent manager—*She watches over the affairs of her household and does not eat the bread of idleness* (verse 27).

She has a godly character—*Charm is deceptive, and beauty is fleeting; but a woman who fears the LORD is to be praised* (verse 30).

Choosing Your Approach to Dating

Wow! This Proverbs lady sounds like a great role model, doesn't she? Do you know anyone like her? Are there girls in your church who have these basic qualities? Well, be patient. She's out there, and God is preparing her for you right now. And He's also busy preparing and perfecting you for a woman like her! In the meantime, here are some choices you need to be making as God gets you ready for the right girl—the best girl—God's girl!

Choose to associate with girls who are active, vibrant, for-real Christians. Start now to develop a list of character qualities from the Bible that are a must for a Christian girl you would spend time with now and want to marry in the future. Then use that list as your guideline for the girls you pal around with today.

You've already looked at the many admirable traits of the woman in Proverbs 31. When you have an opportunity to do so, look at 1 Peter 3:1-6 and Titus 2:3-5 too. You'll see God praising women who are blameless in character and godly in conduct. That's the kind of girl you want to look for. God desires the best for you, and you should desire the best for you too. Don't settle for anyone less than the best.

Choose to focus on group activities rather than on dating or being with an individual girl. Use these group activities (preferably church activities or activities with Christians) to notice the behavior of the girls in your group. Being part of a group also lessens the opportunities for temptations that can come up when you're alone with one girl.

Choose to wait to date seriously until there is a godly purpose or reason—which is marriage. As I said earlier, while you are a teen, what is the purpose of dating? After all, are you planning on getting married anytime soon? Probably not. So, there's no purpose or point in intense dating at this time, even if your motives are pure. Too much seriousness too soon can take you on an emotional roller coaster ride that hurts deeply when it ends, or ruins your reputation, or contributes negatively to your character development, or gets you into sexual trouble and scars you for life.

In the meantime, enjoy being a guy. Enjoy being in middle or high school. Enjoy your guy-friends. And enjoy your gal-friends. Learn to talk to girls and appreciate them. And stay cool. Don't be in a hurry to get serious. Have fun!

Choose to involve your parents. Ask your parents for their advice when it comes to girls. Ask their suggestions on what to look for in a girl. Ask them to help you develop a list of qualities to look for in a girl when the time is right. This is what I did with my daughters when they were young—we talked about desirable qualities in a young man. Believe me, when the emotions came rolling in with what they each thought might be "the one," that list of qualities helped them to think clearly. And your list will help you and your parents to think clearly too when the time comes for more serious relationships. There is a proverb that warns, "It is not good to have zeal without knowledge, nor to be hasty and miss the way" (Proverbs 19:2). Haste only adds to your misery. So don't be in too much of a hurry. Don't miss the way to a pure, guilt-free, happy life.

Choose to remain morally and sexually pure, no matter what!

Make this commitment now, before you start dating. It's a commitment you make between you and God. If you have already started dating, then reaffirm your commitment to God's standard of absolute purity again and again before each date. This is a spiritual choice...and a wise choice...and a right choice. It's choosing whether you're going to follow Jesus or the world. It's choosing whether you are going to follow Jesus or your self—your flesh. And here's a heads up: If your date is trying to tempt you to sin sexually or in any other way, she is absolutely, 100 percent not the girl for you. She's out! This is settled forever. If a girl is godly she will have made her own commitment to God. She will desire sexual purity for herself and for you. And she'll be encouraging your spiritual best, not tempting you to your moral worst.

Oh, and it almost goes without saying, you are not to tempt any girl you date to sin sexually or in any other way!

Choose to be growing spiritually. You might ask how this choice is different from the one you just read. The choice to be pure doesn't require that you be spiritual. There are other "religious" and nonreligious people who believe in sexual abstinence or sexual purity until marriage. They stay sexually pure by sheer willpower. But we are talking about much more than sexual purity. We're talking about becoming a man of God, a man who is pure sexually and will lead his future family in Christian living. This maturity comes from knowing what the Bible teaches, praying to follow it, choosing to obey it, and wanting to live your life God's way.

Making the Tough Choices

The choices you make with regard to dating will be among the most important ones you make in your life. In no way should you approach dating in a casual way. The whole dating experience should be reserved until it's time to begin looking for a life partner.

In the meantime, do your homework. Make a list of the ideal female qualities as stated in the Bible. God's Word has a lot to say about the character of a godly woman. Just be sure you don't confuse *cute* with *character*. Take your time. Study the biblical standard. Ask for God's help as you look for these qualities in the lives of the girls in your church or youth group. And don't forget to ask the advice of your parents! Then, with lots of input, make your list.

Now that you have your "A List," read it over and make it your own. When you see a cute girl and wonder about her, pull out the list. When it's time to think about starting the dating process, pull out the list. When you think you're in love, pull out the list. You'll be glad you have a list of God's standards to use as a guide for choosing the right girl to date.

Meanwhile, while you are waiting and looking, be faithful to prepare yourself so that you too are ready for God's best. Let God work on your character qualities. Be patient, for these qualities take years to develop. As 1 Timothy 6:11 says, "But you, man of God…pursue righteousness, godliness, faith, love, endurance and gentleness." Ask God to help you control your personal purity. Do what is necessary to keep yourself pure in body, soul, mind, and spirit. Then patiently wait for God's best to arrive.

Guy to Guy

Jot down three wrong assumptions—and wrong approaches—
Jason had with regard to dating.

What advice could you give Jason to help him understand the
importance of timing when it comes to dating?

Of all the verses shared in this chapter, which one meant the
most to you that you could pass on to Jason?

In what ways are you like Jason when it comes to a girl, and what
new choices do you need to start making?

Would You Like to Know More?
Check It Out

Look up the verses below in your Bible and note what each one reveals about the quality mentioned. Use these qualities as a guide for your own personal spiritual growth.

Passionate for God—Psalm 63:1

Diligent—Proverbs 12:24

Friendly—Proverbs 17:17

Merciful—Matthew 5:7

Encouraging—Hebrews 3:13

Generous—Proverbs 11:25

Kind—Proverbs 19:17

Discerning—Proverbs 18:15

Faithful—Galatians 5:22-23

God's Guidelines for
Making Right Choices

- *Don't date unbelievers.* "Do not be yoked together with unbelievers…what fellowship can light have with darkness?" (2 Corinthians 6:14).

- *Look for godly qualities.* "Love is patient, love is kind. It does not envy, it does not boast, it is not proud. It is not rude, it is not self-seeking, it is not easily angered, it keeps no record of wrongs…It always protects, always trusts, always hopes, always perseveres" (1 Corinthians 13:4-7).

- *Look for inner character.* "Do not consider his appearance…Man looks at the outward appearance, but the LORD looks at the heart" (1 Samuel 16:7).

- *Look for God's best and nothing less.* "If anything is excellent or praiseworthy—think about such things" (Philippians 4:8).

- *Prepare yourself spiritually.* "This is my prayer: that your love may abound more and more in knowledge and depth of insight, so that you may be able to discern what is best and may be pure and blameless until the day of Christ, filled with the fruit of righteousness that comes through Jesus Christ—to the glory and praise of God" (Philippians 1:9-11).

The Best Time

It's important to realize that love isn't something to play around with. Song of Songs makes that clear when it says, "Do not arouse or awaken love until it so desires" (Song of Songs 2:7). We shouldn't run into a dating relationship simply because everyone else thinks it's OK. God wants us to wait for the right person, not because he doesn't want us to have a good time but because he wants us to have the *best* time.

Because God cares about us so deeply, he wants us to save romantic love for a relationship he would be proud of. We don't know when or if that will happen, but we can trust God to take care of us in his way and in his time.

—Robyn[1]

The Truth About Temptation

*Each of you should learn
to control his own body in a way
that is holy and honorable.*

—1 THESSALONIANS 4:4

As Jason and Mark are dashing down the hall to their English class, Mark blurts out, "Well, are you ready for the big night?" Before Jason could say anything, Mark opens the door to the classroom, and the bell rings.

Jason takes his seat and instantly starts stewing over Mark's question. Jason knows exactly what Mark is talking about. For weeks Jason and Mark had been planning a sleepover at Mark's house. Jason's parents were going away for a night. That meant Jason and his brother and sister were each spending that night with different family friends who had kids their ages.

Jason was going to stay with Mark's family that Friday night. But Jason felt awkward because of an idea Mark had come up with for that evening. Evidently Mark's older brother had a stash of pornographic magazines. Mark knew where they were hidden and thought it would be fun for the two of them to check out the magazines for themselves. And to add to the excitement, Mark had watched his brother go onto several Internet sites with some pretty racy stuff as well. Jason had never done anything like this before, which was making him very nervous. But his curiosity was getting the best of him.

While Jason is pondering this moral dilemma, Mrs. Jones, the English teacher, calls upon Jason to answer a question. As usual, because Jason wasn't listening, he asks her to repeat the question. And, as usual, Jason had no clue about what the answer might be!

A Word About Temptation

Living the Christian life is a struggle. And if you don't think so, then you just might not be living the Christian life! Jesus told His disciples, and you and me, that "in this world you will have trouble" (John 16:33). Some of the trouble Jesus was talking about comes in the form of temptation. For a Christian, the struggle comes when we wrestle with temptation. A temptation itself is not sin, but when you give in to a temptation, it becomes sin. Another problem that comes with temptation is that it comes in a variety of ways and disguises, and the target is always your purity. This is the struggle our friend Jason was facing.

As is the case with all other choices, God expects Jason to choose a biblical approach and manage his temptations in a way that preserves his purity. That sounds like a lot to expect of a young man like Jason, doesn't it? But if you are a Christian, God also expects you to withstand temptation too, no matter what your age. And the best part is that Jesus didn't leave you to manage by yourself. Jesus went on to reassure His disciples, "But take heart! I have overcome the world" (John 16:33). Jesus has promised to help you.

Checking Out God's Word

Temptations that Attack Purity

God has entrusted you with a most important possession—your purity. And with God's help, your purity can be maintained on all levels. As I said, temptations that attack your purity will come in a variety of ways and on a variety of levels. Note the order of the attacks:

Your Spiritual Purity

Temptation on the spiritual level deals with your relationship with God and your heart. When you fail to think seriously and regularly about God and your relationship with Him, and when you fail to value it above all things, you open yourself up to temptation. Notice how many times Satan questioned Eve about God's credibility before she gave in to temptation. Also notice what contributed to Eve's fall in Genesis 3:6. If you have a pen handy, underline the serpent's questions and Eve's answers.

Now the serpent was more crafty than any of the wild animals the LORD God had made. He said to the woman, "Did God really say, 'You must not eat from any tree in the garden'?"

The woman said to the serpent, "We may eat fruit from the trees in the garden, but God did say, 'You must not eat fruit from the tree that is in the middle of the garden, and you must not touch it, or you will die.'"

"You will not surely die," the serpent said to the woman. "For God knows that when you eat of it your eyes will be opened, and you will be like God, knowing good and evil."

When the woman saw that the fruit of the tree was good for food and pleasing to the eye, and also desirable for gaining wisdom, she took some and ate it (Genesis 3:1-6).

Your Mental Purity

All temptation starts with your thoughts. Obviously if your thoughts are pure, your actions will also be pure. Notice what happened with King Saul's thoughts.

The comments of the people—*As they danced, they sang: "Saul has slain his thousands, and David his tens of thousands"* (1 Samuel 18:7).

Saul's reaction—*Saul was very angry; this refrain galled him. "They have credited David with tens of thousands," he thought, "but me with only thousands.*

*What more can he get but the kingdom?" And from
that time on Saul kept a jealous eye on David* (1 Samuel 18:8-9).

The outcome of Saul's impure thoughts—*Saul told
his son Jonathan and all the attendants to kill David*
(1 Samuel 19:1).

What you think is vital to your purity. As Paul stated, you are
to think only on what is true, noble, right, pure, lovely, admirable, excellent, and praiseworthy (Philippians 4:8).

Your Physical Purity

You have a choice about *who* you think about, and *what* you
think about. But once you have entertained wrong thoughts,
then the next natural step, as with King Saul, is to act out your
wrong thoughts in a sinful way. So, to preserve your physical purity, start first with thinking about God. You are always on safe
ground when you are thinking about God, who is holy, holy,
holy. This will fill your mind with pure thoughts, which, in turn,
will guard your physical body.

Joseph is a great example of how a teen boy ought to respond to temptation of a physical nature. Read what happened
to him, and be sure you notice his ultimate reason for not giving in to sin.

*Now Joseph was well-built and handsome, and after
a while his master's wife took notice of Joseph and said,
"Come to bed with me!"*

*But he refused. "With me in charge," he told her, "my
master does not concern himself with anything in the*

house; everything he owns he has entrusted to my care.
No one is greater in this house than I am. My master
has withheld nothing from me except you, because you
are his wife. How then could I do such a wicked thing
and sin against God?" (Genesis 39:6-9)

What a great lesson! If you can only remember one thing
when you are tempted, remember that you don't want to sin
against God.

Thoughts About Purity

When your parents or church youth leaders talk about purity, what are they usually referring to? The physical body, right?
Well, this is the most obvious area and should be discussed, especially because we both know that the temptations you have in
the physical area have their beginning in your mind. God makes
it very clear in the Bible that He wants His people (including
you) to be pure. Do you want to do God's will? If yes, then you
need to read 1 Thessalonians 4:3-5, which mentions one specific
aspect of God's will. Again, if you have your pen handy, you'll
want to underline God's assignments to you.

> *It is God's will that you should be sanctified: that*
> *you should avoid sexual immorality; that each of you*
> *should learn to control your own body in a way that is*
> *holy and honorable, not in passionate lust like the pa-*
> *gans, who do not know God.*

A Christian man, no matter what his age—whether a pre-
teen, a teen, a college student, or a man who has a family—must

pay close attention to protecting his physical purity. The word *pure* has to do with morality. If you look up the word *pure* in a dictionary, you will likely find a definition that speaks of being without stain, free from pollution, clean, innocent, and guilt-less. The same goes for the word *sanctification*. To sanctify yourself means to make yourself holy, to consecrate or dedicate or set yourself apart for God. It describes a condition of being free from sin, of being and standing for what is right and good.

This is heavy stuff, right? But this is God's plan and will for you. So you need to make the choices that will help you stay pure, and then do what is necessary to remain pure in your thoughts and actions. You need to think of yourself as belonging to God. You need to commit yourself to doing what is right and good. Your aim is to be free from sin.

Checking Out God's Word

It's always good to read Scripture because it tells us every-thing we are to think and not think, and everything we are to do and not do. Read the verses below and pay close attention to what they say to you about your purity.

> *Whatever is...pure...think about such things* (Philippians 4:8).

> *Keep yourself pure* (1 Timothy 5:22).

> *Flee the evil desires of youth, and pursue righteousness* (2 Timothy 2:22).

> *To the pure, all things are pure* (Titus 1:15).

This book is entitled *A Young Man's Guide to Making Right Choices*. As you know by now, it's about the choices you could make, the choices you should make, the choices you do make, and the results of those choices. Some time ago I read a quote from a professor at Moody Bible Institute, who said, "Character is the sum and total of a person's choices."[1] Think about his words as you read about some of the choices that are yours to make each day regarding your purity. Below are some verses you may remember having already seen, but that's a good thing. Repetition helps make God's Word stay hidden in your heart.

Choose godliness—The first and foremost step in maintaining your purity is to run away from sin and pursue a life of godliness.

> *You, man of God, flee from all this [a life of sin], and pursue righteousness, godliness, faith, love, endurance and gentleness* (1 Timothy 6:11).

Choose to avoid places and situations where you might be tempted—Paul told his young friend Timothy to "flee the evil desires of youth" (2 Timothy 2:22). This is powerful advice for Jason as he considers the activities that Mark has planned for the sleepover at his house. Follow Joseph's example when a temptation comes along—run away from temptation, and do so immediately!

Choose to avoid people who might tempt you—I hope you remember reading earlier that you are not to make friends with people who pull you down and away from God's standards. Unfortunately, Jason probably didn't have a choice about staying overnight at Mark's house. But he did have a choice about being influenced by Mark to do something he knew was wrong. And so do you. All you have to do is say no.

If sinners entice you, do not give in to them...do not go along with them, do not set foot on their paths (Proverbs 1:10,15).

Making the Tough Choices

Maybe you don't think purity is such a big deal. And that's exactly what the devil and the world want you to think. But purity is a big deal—a huge deal! Why? Because it affects your relationship with God. God is pure and demands that His children be pure too. So the next time you have impure thoughts, or are tempted to do some impure act, think about your relationship with Jesus.

And here's another important fact: Purity is related to your personal character. When you are morally pure at the core of your being, purity will show up in your thoughts, words, and deeds. Your daily actions of self-restraint will honor God and give others no reason for thinking anything other than the best of you.

As the apostle Paul said, "Keep yourself pure." And let me add: Keep yourself pure *always*. Purity isn't something you struggle with only while you are a young man. Purity is a lifelong challenge, a lifelong calling, and a lifelong issue of your heart. Your behavior will always be determined by where your heart is set. So do whatever you must to make sure your heart's compass is set toward God and the purity He desires of you.

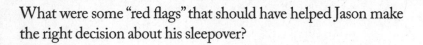

Guy to Guy

What were some "red flags" that should have helped Jason make the right decision about his sleepover?

What principles could you give Jason to help him understand the importance of upholding God's standards of purity?

Of all the verses shared in this chapter, which one meant the most to you that you could pass on to Jason?

In what ways are you like Jason, and what new choices do you need to start making?

Would You Like to Know More?
Check It Out

The apostle Paul tells us that we are to glorify and honor God with our bodies. Read 1 Corinthians 6:13-20 with your bodily purity in view.

Verse 13—What is totally off limits when it comes to how you use your body?

Instead, how are you to use your body?

Verse 15—What question does this verse ask?

Since this is true, what else is totally off limits to you (verses 15-16)?

Verse 17—Describe the relationship you enjoy when you are united with Christ.

Verse 18—What is the command?

Why is this important?

Verse 19—What question is asked in this verse?

And what fact is given?

Verse 20—To whom do you belong, and why?

Because of your relationship with Christ, what are you commanded to do?

God's Guidelines for
Making Right Choices

- *Go to God for the strength you need.* "Those who hope in the LORD will renew their strength. They will soar on wings like eagles; they will run and not grow weary, they will walk and not be faint" (Isaiah 40:31).

- *Go to God's Word for the growth and wisdom you need.* "Like newborn babies, crave pure spiritual milk, so that by it you may grow up in your salvation" (1 Peter 2:2).

- *Go to God for the control you need.* "The fruit of the Spirit is love, joy, peace, patience, kindness, goodness, faithfulness, gentleness and self-control" (Galatians 5:22-23).

- *Go to God for help in being an example.* "Don't let anyone look down on you because you are young, but set an example for the believers in speech, in life, in love, in faith and in purity" (1 Timothy 4:12).

- *Go to God for victory.* "Thanks be to God! He gives us the victory through our Lord Jesus Christ" (1 Corinthians 15:57).

Second Chances

*Trust in the LORD with all your heart
and lean not on your own understanding;
in all your ways acknowledge him,
and he will make your paths straight.*

—PROVERBS 3:5-6

Jason felt like a real failure. It had been a really bad week. He seemed to have made all the wrong choices all week long, which continued on into Friday when he chose to give in to the temptation to cheat on his history test.

And then there was Friday night at Mark's house. Jason had caved in to Mark's plan. Rather than say no, he chose to follow along. He and Mark had the full experience, complete with graphic pictures. He knew it was wrong the whole time he was looking, but he just couldn't seem to help himself. Worse than viewing the images was the fact that, even after the escapade was over, he still had those images in his mind. Every time he tried to forget, they popped back into his mind. Talk about a nightmare! No, Jason would never forget that night—in more than one way.

And now it's Sunday. And Jason is still reliving that horrible night of making poor choices as he slowly slides into a chair in the back row of his youth group class at church. Feeling utterly defeated and dejected, he knew he could never tell his parents about what he had done. They would completely freak out! And he just didn't think he could handle how disappointed they would be because of his actions. What a failure—he was so ashamed! Yes, he knew he had reached his all-time low.

Jason felt as if he were going crazy. *How can I ever look at a girl again?* he thought. *Those images have really messed me up. And what about my youth pastor, Rick? If he ever found out, he'd be really disappointed too.* Jason was struggling with these thoughts as the group began the class with singing.

But Jason knows he has a much deeper issue to come to grips with: How can he face Jesus after having messed up so badly? Surely Jesus was disappointed in him. And how can he keep from making other awful decisions in the future? Poor Jason. For once, his sorrow was real and heartfelt.

About this time Pastor Rick got up, prayed, and began to teach from Proverbs 3:5-6.

Choosing Whether You Are In or Out

Jason had always lived on the fringe of his Christian friends and their circle. It was his choice, of course. Sure, he always went to youth group. (His parents made sure of that!) But he never tuned in to what was happening there. Instead, he lived with one foot in the world and one foot in the Christian scene.

But on this miserable, memorable day, Jason was living with some horrific regrets. Suddenly he had a desperate need for help and answers. He knew in his heart that he had made a choice to dabble in worldly ways, and now he was tasting the results of that choice.

Jason knew he had to make another decision—he had to get out of the world and dive headlong and wholeheartedly toward Jesus. Maybe, just maybe, something Pastor Rick said today might help! So for the first time in a l-o-n-g time, Jason made an effort to listen—to really, really listen.

Choosing to Trust God

Also, for the first time in a long time, Jason had brought his Bible to the meeting. He was glad he had done so because Pastor Rick (as always) began class by saying, "Open your Bibles." Then he added, "Turn with me to Proverbs 3, and let's take a look at verses 5 and 6." Jason opened his Bible right away and read the fantastic truths in those passages. Help was on the way!

Trust in the LORD with all your heart (verse 5)—Do you ever feel like there's no one you can trust? That there's no one who understands what you're feeling when you have an important decision to make? It's awful to feel so alone! Your parents don't always relate. Your friends are little or no help. You feel like the weight of the world is on your shoulders. So you sort of half-pray, "If there was just someone I could talk to…Someone I could trust with my problems and decisions…"

And when your list comes up empty, you decide there isn't anyone who can help you. So you make your choice alone, without any input from others. Sometimes your choice is okay. But sometimes (like Jason's Friday night disaster!) it leads to calamity.

You know what I'm about to say next, don't you? Yes, there *is* someone you can trust 100 percent of the time with 100 percent of the choices you must make. That someone is God. And God knows 100 percent of the time what is 100 percent best for you. He's a better judge of what's right, and what you need, and what's good or harmful for you than you are. In fact, He's the best!

You already know all this, don't you? But now it's time for you to truly believe it and apply it in your life. In every choice you make, from the small ones to the monumental ones, you must completely trust and believe that God can—and will—help you make the right choice. That's where "with all your heart" (verse 5) comes in. Can you do that? You will never know God's will completely without trusting Him to help you in your decision making.

Lean not on your own understanding (verse 5)—God isn't asking you to give up your ability to think and reason. But He is asking you to listen to the wisdom of His Word, to your conscience, and to the prompting of His Spirit, not to mention to the wisdom of your parents and church leaders.

You see, this was Jason's problem. He wanted what he wanted. And he was listening to the wrong advice and following the wrong people. He was listening to everyone but God. He was totally excluding God and the resources God had given him (like His Word and prayer) when it came to making choices. Jason was very much leaning on his own understanding.

Take, for instance, Jason's decision to look at those magazines and Internet sites. If only he had followed his conscience, he wouldn't have ended up making the wrong choice. The fact he felt nervous should have been a big red flag! He could have reached out for help from God, from his parents, and from his youth pastor or other wise Christians. As the Bible says, God always provides a way out of your temptation:

> *No temptation has seized you except what is common to man. And God is faithful; he will not let you be tempted beyond what you can bear. But when you are tempted, he will also provide a way out so that you can stand up under it* (1 Corinthians 10:13).

God's way out of temptation could have come through any of the people who would have guided Jason to the right decision. If Jason had only stopped, paid attention to his inner self—his heart and conscience—waited, prayed, listened to God and His people, and trusted in God's wisdom, he would have been spared of his painful experience and its far-reaching consequences.

In all your ways acknowledge him (verse 6)—How do you acknowledge the presence of a friend? You call out his name. You wave. You flash a smile and yell out a greeting. You give him a high five. Well, acknowledging God is no different. You've already established that Jesus is your best friend, right? He's always there, and He will never leave or forsake you or turn on you. So, make sure you're always acknowledging His presence in your life.

The best way to recognize God's presence is through prayer. Just bring your every decision to Jesus in prayer. Involve Him. Let Him help with your choices. Every one of them is important to Him...and should be to you too. He wants you to acknowledge your need for His divine advice. Just pray with a sincere heart, "What shall I do, Lord?" (Acts 22:10).

He will make your paths straight (verse 6)—Like Jason, you need to examine your values. Everyone needs to do this, and do it often. Just don't be a Jason. Don't wait until you're backed into a corner or after you've made some terrible mistake. Ask yourself questions like these *before* you make a wrong choice:

- What's really important to me, and are these same areas important to God?
- What are my priorities? Or rather, what should they be?
- Have I fully given my heart to Jesus, and am I living like it?

You may already be acknowledging God in many areas of your life. That's the way it should be. But maybe you need to dig deeper and ask these questions as well:

- Are there any areas of my life I'm holding onto for myself and withholding from God?
- Am I keeping God at arm's length in an attempt to restrict or ignore His involvement in my life?

Putting God at the center of your life will assure His guidance in the choices you make. As you can see, according to Proverbs 3:6, your job is to acknowledge God in everything and seek His will. Once you do that, His job is to direct and guide you—to make your paths obvious and straight. He will clear out the roadblocks, remove the hurdles, and enable you to move confidently forward toward His will. As that happens, you'll find yourself making the right choices, which means you'll enjoy life more and suffer less. Why? Because you'll be intent on working with God to accomplish His purposes. How cool is that?

Checking Out God's Word

What is the result of trusting in the Lord with all your heart? If your pen is handy, grab it and make these truths your own. Jot down your favorite part of each verse.

Seek first his kingdom and his righteousness, and all these things will be given to you as well (Matthew 6:33).

Do not conform any longer to the pattern of this world, but be transformed by the renewing of your mind. Then you will be able to test and approve what God's will is—His good, pleasing and perfect will (Romans 12:2).

I will instruct you and teach you in the way you should go; I will counsel you and watch over you (Psalm 32:8).

If any of you lacks wisdom, he should ask God, who gives generously to all without finding fault, and it will be given to him (James 1:5).

Knowing About God's Forgiveness

As Jason listened to Pastor Rick, he realized he had heard the answer he was looking for. It was as if a light had turned on. And it was so simple! All he had to do was choose to trust God with every detail of his life, and God would help him make the right choices. (Of course, we all know this is easier said than done, but Jason got it!)

But there was still one problem: Jason's sin. He looked back on all he had done over the past week and sighed. *I did so many things wrong this last week. How can I make a fresh start? How can I get my life turned around? How could God ever forgive me?*

Well, God came to the rescue again. And He used Pastor Rick, who seemed to be reading Jason's mind as he went on to explain forgiveness from Ephesians 1:7:

> *In [Jesus] we have redemption through his blood, the forgiveness of sins, in accordance with the riches of God's grace.*

God is 100 percent holy, and He cannot associate with sin. And because all people are sinful, all people are separated from God. The bad news is that because of our sin, we deserve punishment and death. But the good news is that because of Jesus' death on the cross, we can be spared from spiritual death if we accept, by faith, Jesus' death in our place. We can receive forgiveness for our sins.

Pastor Rick then gave a simple prayer for those who had not yet received God's gift of forgiveness. As he did so, he let them know the prayer must come from their heart:

> Jesus, I know I am a sinner. I want to repent of my

sins and turn and follow You. I believe You died for my sins and rose again victorious over the power of sin and death, and I want to accept You as my personal Savior. Come into my life, Lord Jesus, and help me obey You from this day forward. Amen.

Jason prayed along with Pastor Rick, just in case he wasn't saved, just in case he wasn't really a Christian at all. In his heart he truly believed that Jesus was his Savior. But, after this last week, Jason was unsure of where he stood with God, so he wanted to be sure. He knew his sins had been forgiven when he committed his life to Jesus. He already belonged to Jesus. That wasn't his problem. His problem was himself—his personal, ongoing, daily sin. And Jason had to admit, it did seem to be getting worse.

I know that Jesus died on the cross for my sins. But how could Jesus forgive all the awful sins I've committed this past week? Jason agonized. *I neglected God. I was lazy and selfish. I was horrible to my family for no reason at all. I purposefully went against my parents' rules and wishes. I cheated. And I willingly participated in some awful stuff that was actually planned in advance!*

Again, God came to Jason's aid. It was truly as if Pastor Rick again anticipated Jason's questions. This time Rick had everyone open their Bibles to 1 John 1:9:

> *If we confess our sins, he is faithful and just and will forgive us our sins and purify us from all unrighteousness.*

Pastor Rick explained that because of the sacrifice Jesus Christ made on the cross, Jason's salvation came with unlimited grace from God. Therefore Jason's problem (and yours) with ongoing, daily sin was solved by Jesus and because of Jesus! Pastor

Rick explained that as believers acknowledge their sin (which Jason quickly did), they can be assured of God's ongoing willingness to give ongoing forgiveness.

And yes, Pastor Rick had another prayer for the group to consider—a prayer of recommitment. Jason didn't miss a second even thinking about whether or not he would pray this prayer! No, this one was just for him. He prayed these words with all his heart as Pastor Rick said them:

> Jesus, I know that in the past I asked You into my life. I thought, at that time, that I was Your child, but my life hasn't shown the fruit of my belief. As I again hear Your call, I want to make a real commitment to You as the Lord and Master of my life. I want to know that I am Your child—and live like it. Amen.

What freedom! Jason's burden of his failure to live for Jesus was lifted. His confession left him knowing and feeling the cleansing power of Jesus as it washed over him. He was clean from the past—and the past week!—and was eager to move forward with living for Jesus.

Forgetting What Lies Behind

Isn't God great? He has given you and me the gift of salvation through His Son, who keeps forgiving even when we sin after becoming a believer. With that in mind, perhaps you are wondering, like Jason, *How can I move on after I've failed?*

If anyone had a good reason to regret some horrible things he'd done in his life, it was the apostle Paul. Before he met Jesus, Paul helped stone to death a righteous man named Stephen

(Acts 7:59–8:1). He also played a major role in the persecution of many Christians (Acts 9:1-2).

Can you imagine how Paul felt when Jesus brought him to his knees and gave him complete and unconditional forgiveness (Acts 9:1-5)? But one thing Paul knew was that he had to move on and serve God with his whole heart from that day on. No more wasted days. No more wasted life. Oh, to be sure, Paul probably had regrets and felt deep sorrow over his past actions. But he could also say,

> *Forgetting what is behind and straining toward what is ahead, I press on toward the goal to win the prize for which God has called me heavenward in Christ Jesus* (Philippians 3:13-14).

Like Paul, you must make a choice about your past. You must choose to accept God's forgiveness. And you must choose to remember that forgiveness every time you are tempted to recall your past failures. Like Paul, you must choose to forget the past and press on toward the future. This, my friend, is what will enable you to face each day and the coming years with excitement and joyful expectation of what God has prepared for you.

Making the Tough Choices

How often do people give you a second chance? Sometimes not very often, right? But God does! His ongoing forgiveness offers you a second, third, fourth, and many more chances. All you have to do is come to Him with a repentant heart every time you sin.

But a word of caution: The sorrow you express over the sins you've committed must be genuine. So be sure you examine your heart. Ask yourself, "What is my sorrow based on? Am I sorry only because I got caught, or am I truly sorry for giving in to temptation? Am I sorry for disappointing people, or sorry for disappointing God?" Whenever you come to God, come with a completely exposed heart. He delights in giving you and your heart a thorough cleansing.

And here's an encouraging thought about moving on: If you've strayed and taken the wrong path, you can start walking on a new and right path—God's path—anytime. And even if the consequences of your sin are ongoing, God can and will give you the grace and strength to do what is necessary to make things right and help you live with the consequences of your actions. You can do everything—including moving on, including turning your life around—through Christ, who gives you strength (Philippians 4:13).

Guy to Guy

Jot down several right choices that Jason had finally made. What important corners does he seem to have turned?

What comfort and words of encouragement could you give Jason as you sit next to him in the youth group?

Of all the verses shared in this chapter, which one meant the most to you that you could share with Jason, and why?

In what ways are you like Jason, and what actions do you need to take about some of the bad choices you've made, about turning your life around?

Would You Like to Know More?
Check It Out

What do you learn about God's forgiveness in the following verses?

Isaiah 1:18—

Psalm 103:12—

Matthew 26:28—

Acts 10:43—

1 John 1:9—

It's been said that those who are forgiven much forgive much. What do these verses say about the kind of attitude you should have when it comes to forgiving others?

Matthew 18:21-22—

Acts 7:59-60—

Ephesians 4:32—

Colossians 3:12-13—

Try your hand at writing a brief prayer of thanks to Jesus for all He's done for you, is doing in you, and will be faithful to do for you in the future.

God's Guidelines for Making Right Choices

- *You are known and special to God.* "Before I formed you in the womb I knew you, before you were born I set you apart" (Jeremiah 1:5).

- *You are loved by God, and His Son died for your sins.* "God demonstrates his own love for us in this: While we were still sinners, Christ died for us" (Romans 5:8).

- *You are accepted and blessed of God through His Son.* "Praise be to the God and Father of our Lord Jesus Christ, who has blessed us in the heavenly realms with every spiritual blessing in Christ" (Ephesians 1:3).

- *You are complete in Christ.* "In Christ all the fullness of the Deity lives in bodily form, and you have been given fullness in Christ, who is the head over every power and authority" (Colossians 2:9-10).

- *You are a work in progress and will one day be perfect.* "[Be] confident of this, that he who began a good work in you will carry it on to completion until the day of Christ Jesus" (Philippians 1:6).

You Can Do It!

One thing I do:
Forgetting what is behind and
straining toward what is ahead, I press on
toward the goal to win the prize for which
God has called me heavenward in Christ.

—PHILIPPIANS 3:13-14

Have you ever asked for "do overs" when you were playing some sport? I have done that plenty of times while playing golf with my closest friends. Because they are my friends, they willingly let me take a shot again, and I do the same for them. They give me a second chance to get it right. And would you believe that most of the time, I make a much better shot! I do better the second time around. Well, that's exactly how Jason felt as he sat on his bed the Sunday afternoon after his disastrous week. And it was a good feeling. Sundays are meant to be special, and this one truly was!

"Today is the first day of the rest of your life" was Pastor Rick's comment as he closed his time with the youth group that morning. As Jason sat thinking, he realized he had been greatly helped by Rick's teaching about choosing to trust God. Wow, what a jolt! And what a blessing. Rick's lesson from God's Word had truly been life-changing.

Pastor Rick had also touched on forgiveness. Jason felt like this was truly the first day of the rest of his life. He had been given a "do over" by God! And much to his surprise, Jason had also benefitted from the sermon given during the morning worship service. In the past he had always tuned out the senior pastor during the church service. Jason always found himself distracted during church…he would doodle, count the tiles in the ceiling, text his friends, and think about what computer game he was going to play when he got home.

But today—well, it was like he had new ears. This morning, Dr. Gray's message was very helpful, even for a teenager. *Wow,* thought Jason, *that sermon today was really awesome. It spoke to me. I felt like the pastor was talking right to me. How did both he and Pastor Rick know exactly what I needed to hear?* (In fact, during the service, Jason never thought once about what computer game he was going to play when he got home!)

Your Life God's Way

If you will look at the cover of this book, you'll see that the subtitle is *Your Life God's Way.* That's what making right choices will do for you. And that's where we find Jason this Sunday afternoon.

Can you believe all that has happened to Jason in only a few hours? His entire life has turned a corner and taken a new, fantastic, and exciting direction. Even Jason could hardly believe that he was ready to do serious business with God. But oh, was he ever! He was eager to start fresh with his life. It's one thing to know what's right…and an entirely different thing to actually do and live what's right, to live life God's way.

Yes, Jason had determined that things were definitely going to be different—way different. They had to be! Let's face it—his life was an utter mess. Sheer chaos. He never wanted to live another week like last week. He was carefully—even with some prayers thrown in—mulling over the new commitments and decisions he was making, choices that would demonstrate the life-changing decisions he'd made that morning in youth group.

And to doubly ensure that he didn't fall back into his old ways and habits, Jason asked Pastor Rick to help him out by checking up on him each week at the study. Then to make his commitment even stronger, Jason had asked Isaac and Ryan to hold him accountable. These two guys were in his youth group and also went to his school. They seemed to have their act together and demonstrated a strong witness at school. They were thrilled and both agreed to stand with him, pray for him, and check up on his faithfulness to his new commitments. Jason thought, *It's as if I'm getting two new friends—real friends who want to follow God and want His best for me!*

Starting Fresh

"Now, let's get this fresh start thing going," Jason said to himself as he looked at the books and papers spread out across his bed. "Bible…check. Notebook with Pastor Rick's notes from this morning…check. Prayer notebook…check." Jason was ready to take Pastor Rick's advice and follow some of the principles he had outlined for the group. "Let's see…What did Rick say about living—really living—for Jesus? Oh yeah, here it is. He gave us a checklist."

Daily Checklist for a Young Man Who Desires to Live for Jesus

✓ *Start with God*—Spend time in God's Word. "Either sin will keep you from this Book, or this Book will keep you from sin."

✓ *Don't forget to include prayer.* Pray for yourself, your day, your family members, your attitude, your friends, your walk with God, and your purity.

✓ *Act like a child of the King,* which includes how you dress, talk, and treat your family.

✓ *Choose your friends carefully.* In the words of George Washington, "It is better to be alone than in bad company."

✓ *Do things right.* Do all things to the glory of God (Colossians 3:23). That includes your school work, chores, and activities.

✓ *Be smart when it comes to dating.* Don't be afraid to wait to date, to hold out for the right kind of girl and to involve your parents.

✓ *Be accountable to others for your purity.* Stay pure at all costs. It's better to be less popular and less experienced than to be sorry.

After Jason read through Pastor Rick's daily checklist again, he suddenly knew how he should spend the rest of his day. Instead of playing computer games by himself, he could spend some time downstairs with his family. He could start on his homework. He could give his schoolwork the attention it deserved (and needed!) to do it well…to do it for the Lord, not for his parents or teachers. He could even work in advance on some of his projects and papers. Oh, and he could even get a head start on his lesson for his Bible study group. Why, he could even clean up his room!

And Jason made a mental note to himself: He also needed to go through his closet and make sure he had an appropriate T-shirt for school tomorrow. He determined to throw away those that gave the wrong message for a guy who was a Christian. Maybe he'd even wear the one he got last summer at church camp that made a bold statement about Jesus!

Oh, and he definitely needed to decide when he was going to wake up. He wanted to begin his fresh new life and his fresh new day with God. To pray about his life and his day. To be a better son and brother, maybe even help out his family members before school, especially his little brother and sister. To eat a better breakfast, and, oh yes, to get to the bus a little early. *Boy, will Mrs. Bradford be surprised!*

Jesus is not a magic fix for life. No, as Jason begins his fresh and revised journey with Jesus there will be many tough decisions that he will have to make. But Jesus has given some very black-and-white answers to making the right choices on many issues. Read on. If your answer is no to any of these "no-brainers," then it's not a direction you should take.

Certain Choices Are "No-brainers"

1. Is it legal?

Live such good lives among the pagans that, though they accuse you of doing wrong, they may see your good deeds and glorify God on the day he visits us (1 Peter 2:12).

2. Will my parents approve?

Children, obey your parents in the Lord, for this is right (Ephesians 6:1).

3. Will it cause others to stumble?

When you sin against your brothers in this way and wound their weak conscience, you sin against Christ. Therefore, if what I eat causes my brother to fall into sin, I will never eat meat again, so that I will not cause him to fall (1 Corinthians 8:12-13).

4. Will it benefit others? Is it profitable?

"Everything is permissible for me"—but not everything is beneficial (1 Corinthians 6:12).

5. Will it become habit forming?

"Everything is permissible for me"—but I will not be mastered by anything (1 Corinthians 6:12).

6. Will it edify?

"Everything is permissible"—but not everything is beneficial (1 Corinthians 10:23).

7. Will it be a good testimony to the world?

It is God's will that by doing good you should silence the ignorant talk of foolish men (1 Peter 2:15).

8. Will it glorify God?

Whether you eat or drink or whatever you do, do it all for the glory of God (1 Corinthians 10:31).

Making the Tough Choices

You, my friend, have a wonderful and full life. These are exciting days for you. And I know we haven't covered all the areas and issues of your life. But I hope and pray you have glimpsed at least a portion of how important making right choices is each and every day. That's how you live life God's way, and it's done one choice at a time. Here's how I look at it:

Life is but a string of daily choices.
And the best life consists of the best choices,
which are usually the tough choices.

This means that each day is vitally important. Each day you can choose to…live a day for Jesus:

> live a day of order
>
> live a day of walking in the Spirit
>
> live a day of making right choices

Or you can choose not to. To help you make good, better, and best choices, on page 189 you will find a list titled "Seven Steps to Making Right Choices." It's short and to the point. You can refer to it each time you're faced with having to make a choice. Copy the list. Share it. Put a copy on your bathroom mirror and inside your locker door at school. Do whatever you have to do to make sure you use it!

As you finish this book—and start putting God's plan for you into action—send up a prayer to God. Ask Him to help you commit to making the choices that will create a better life for you. Think about the principles and guidelines that have been shared in this book. Then purpose to put them to work in your life…beginning today. You'll begin to experience what the apostle Paul meant when he declared, "To live is Christ" (Philippians 1:21).

Seven Steps to Making Right Choices

1. *Stop*—Don't rush your decisions. As the saying goes, "Fools rush in."

2. *Pause*—It's better to miss an opportunity than get into something that harms you or dishonors God.

3. *Pray*—Through prayer, settle in your heart that you truly want to do the right thing, to make the right choice. Ask God for wisdom. He's promised to give it to you (James 1:5).

4. *Search the Bible*—God's Word is God's guidebook. Everything you need for making the best choices is in Scripture.

5. *Seek advice*—Once you've stopped, waited, prayed, and searched the Scriptures, it never hurts to ask a trusted friend if the choice you're about to make is the best choice.

6. *Act*—Make a decision. Once you have gone through steps 1 to 5 and have the information you need, then in faith and the assurance that you've been careful, go ahead and make your decision.

7. *Proceed*—Don't lose your nerve. You've put in time, prayer, and study into your decision. Follow through on your wise choice—and make any necessary adjustments along the way.

Notes

Making the Right Choices

1. Roy B. Zuck, *The Speaker's Quote Book* (Grand Rapids, MI: Kregel, 1997), p. 110.
2. Neil S. Wilson, ed., *The Handbook of Bible Application* (Wheaton, IL: Tyndale House, 2000), pp. 86-87.

Choice #1: Daylight's a Burning!

1. *Teen Esteem* as quoted in Roy B. Zuck, *The Speaker's Quote Book* (Grand Rapids, MI: Kregel, 1997), p. 165.
2. Derek Kidner, *The Proverbs* (Downers Grove, IL: InterVarsity, 1973), pp. 42-43.
3. John Piper, *Don't Waste Your Life* (Wheaton, IL: Crossway, 2003), back cover.

Choice #2: Getting Your Marching Orders

1. *God's Words of Life for Teens* (Grand Rapids, MI: Zondervan, 2000), p. 29.

Choice #3: Knowing the Game Plan

1. John Piper, *Don't Waste Your Life* (Wheaton, IL: Crossway, 2003), back cover.
2. Excerpted from Elizabeth George, *A Young Woman's Call to Prayer* (Eugene OR: Harvest House, 2005), pp. 25-33.
3. Joe White and Jim Weidmann, gen. eds., citing Nanci Hellmich, "A Teen Thing: Losing Sleep," *USA Today* (May 28, 2000), *Parent's Guide to the Spiritual Mentoring of Teens* (Wheaton, IL: Tyndale House, 2001), p. 447.
4. Jim George, *The Bare Bones Bible® Handbook for Teens* (Eugene, OR: Harvest House, 2008), p. 79.

Choice #4: The Golden Rule Begins at Home

1. *Life Application Bible* (Wheaton, IL: Tyndale House, 1988), p. 1339.

Choice #5: Where's My Favorite T-shirt?

1. Curtis Vaughan, gen. ed., *The Word—the Bible from 26 Translations*, (Grand Rapids, MI: Baker, 1985), quoting *The New Testament: A Translation in the Language of the People* by Charles B. Williams (Gulfport, MS: Mathis Publishers, 1993), p. 2273.

Choice #7: The Road to Success

1. Adapted from Sterling W. Sill, cited in Paul Lee Tan, *Encyclopedia of 7700 Illustrations* (Winona Lake, IN: BMH Books, 1979), pp. 723-34.

Choice #9: What About Girls?

1. *God's Words of Life for Teens* (Grand Rapids, MI: Zondervan, 2000), p. 33.

Choice #10: The Truth About Temptation

1. P.B. Fitzwater. Unfortunately the resource in which I found this quote is unknown, but I had memorized it because it had such an impact on me.